CYRIL ~MEDITH B

George and Florence Adrian

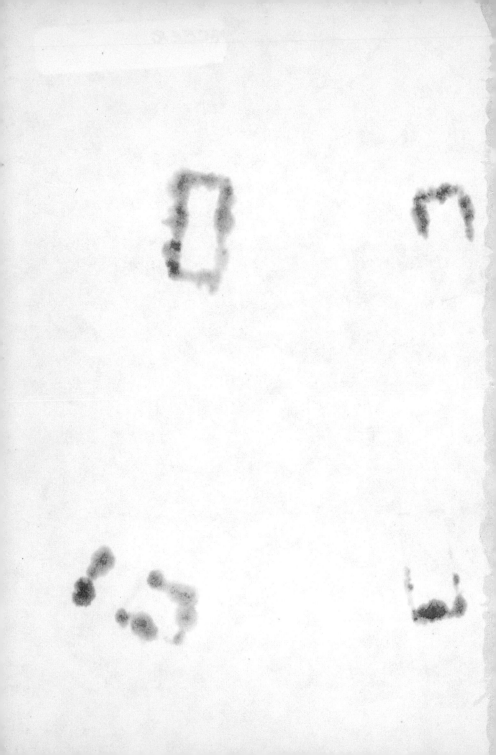

TAUGHT by the MASTER

TAUGHT
by the
MASTER

Clarence W. Cranford

BROADMAN PRESS
Nashville, Tennessee

Library of Congress Card Catalog Number: 56–10284

Printed in the United States of America

5.AL56 K.S.P.

CONTENTS

CONTENTS

FOREWORD

~~~~~~

Some years ago a noted European who had visited America was asked what impressed him most about life in the United States. To the questioner's surprise the European replied, "They get their children together in small groups and teach them Bible stories." What to many today seems an innocuous procedure was, in the eyes of this visitor, a matter of genuine significance. The part which Bible teaching has played in forming and maintaining our principles and ideals as a nation cannot be lightly estimated. The army of men and women who, Sunday after Sunday, without pay or much recognition, gather in our Sunday schools and give of their time and energy to teach Bible truths to squirming, but impressionable, children, to youth and adults, is making a contribution to the moral idealism of our country far in excess of what most people realize.

The inspiration comes from the master Teacher himself. We cannot give too much attention to the message of Jesus or to the methods by which he presented it. He has something to say to our world. In a large sense, he himself is that message. But he wants us to tell the message of his life and love to a confused and sinful world. To tell it more effectively, we need to study carefully what he said and how he said it.

Recognizing the vital role of Christian teaching, and especially that played by church school teachers everywhere, many of the Washington churches have, for several years, held what they call "A Christian School in the Nation's Capital." Each year, in a series held on successive Tuesday evenings, some twelve to fifteen hundred church school teachers and workers meet together for study and inspiration. In addition to classes on methods and Bible study, there is presented each year by one of the local clergy a series of lectures on some theme suggested by the committee that plans and promotes the school. The theme suggested for this series was, "Jesus, the Master Teacher." It developed into the theme, "The Peerless Teacher Speaks to Perilous Times." Somewhat revised and amplified, these lectures are presented here, not for theological experts, but for ordinary Christian laymen and workers in the hope that they may give some inspiration for what the author considers one of the most significant roles anyone can play—that of teaching the Bible and its undying truths to a religiously illiterate generation.

The purpose is frankly inspirational. It is hoped that something in these pages will turn the reader back to a new study of the Gospels themselves, and to him who is the master Teacher of all times.

TAUGHT by the MASTER

I.
THE MASTER TEACHER
FOR OUR TIMES

~~~~~~~~~~

It was a great moment in the history of man's religious quest when Nicodemus, a ruler of the Jews, set out through the night to seek an interview with Jesus. How little he realized as he walked along in the darkness that his visit was to make religious history and become the means of opening new vistas of truth and understanding to succeeding generations of seekers after God! And how little he realized, too, that in a few minutes he would hear words that would revolutionize his, and mankind's, concept of religion! For he who could pride himself on the rich religious heritage into which he had been born and in which he had distinguished himself as a Pharisee and a leader of the Jews, would be told he must be born again.

Born again when already one is old? This would be puzzling doctrine to understand and accept—especially for one who could claim to be an heir of the promise made to Abraham. And yet Jesus' words would clearly indicate that one's acceptance into the kingdom of God calls for a new beginning. It is not something one can inherit, but must experience. It does not depend on what man can do, but on what God is able to accomplish in the human heart. It calls for such a complete reorientation of life that Jesus likened it to a new birth.

God, not man, is the initiator of this new life. Love,

1

not law, is its basis. Jesus is its mediator. He came to reveal it and to make it available for every man. Its promise is not limited to any race or nation. Its rewards outlast the limits of time itself. The primary factor in bringing this new birth about is God's own Spirit, which, like the blowing of the wind, is invisible, but real.

Thus he whose thoughts must have been primarily concerned with the nation (undoubtedly, one of the things that led him to seek Jesus was to learn, if possible, Jesus' plans for Israel) would be made to think primarily of himself and of the changes that needed to be made in his own life and faith before Israel could become the kind of a nation God wanted it to be. For God's kind of a kingdom cannot be superimposed, even by divine power, upon a self-righteous, unrepentant people, but must develop from within the hearts and lives of those who have been led into a personal awareness of his redemptive love, and who seek to share that love in their relationships with all mankind.

The Christian world is indebted to Nicodemus and his nocturnal visit to Jesus for two reasons: It was not only in response to his quest and need that Jesus uttered some of his most penetrating insights into the nature and scope of the Christian gospel as he pointed out God's redemptive concern for Israel and the entire world, but Nicodemus himself contributed one of the most striking compliments to Jesus to be found in the pages of the Gospels. Whether with sincerity or a mere studied attempt to flatter Jesus, he addressed him with the salutation, "Rabbi, we know that thou art a teacher come from God: for no man can do these miracles that thou doest, except God be with him." [1] In so addressing Jesus, Nicodemus has given us a phrase to ponder, for Jesus did choose the role of a teacher; and yet he claimed to speak with unqualified authority concerning the true meaning and purpose of life and the nature of the Power that lies back of this universe.

In these days of multiple voices when so many conflicting ideas and opinions are being expressed and seek to capture the minds of men, we need to give renewed attention to the words of Jesus and to consider carefully his approach to men's hearts and minds. Therefore, the story of Nicodemus takes on new significance in our time. The haunting picture of his lonely figure moving through the shadowy night has become a kind of a symbol of our age; for today all civilization is hastening through a night of confusion and fear—whether to destruction or to the dawn of a new day, we cannot say. Much depends upon the direction of men's quest. If their desperation leads them to Jesus and his insights, there is hope for mankind. But if they continue to rely upon the dictates of their own cleverness and pride, then the future looks dark indeed. For men, now armed with the means of mass destruction too horrible to contemplate, still need to be reborn; to be released from the vindictiveness and pride that have kept them from achieving the peace which they seek.

When Jesus stood in the presence of those who clamored for his death, and Pilate sought to reason with them concerning Jesus' innocence, the Book says, "The voices of them and of the chief priests prevailed." [2]

The wrong voices still prevail today. In many parts of the world, the voice of truth and reason is being drowned out by the raucous cries of dictators. On a world front communism dins its false promises into the ears of hundreds of millions, while here in the United States millions seem to listen only to the enticing voices of those who promise them creature comforts and sensate pleasure. The call to faith in spiritual power has little chance to be heard against the volume of words that pour from the throats of the so-called realists who put their trust almost wholly in material resources and in the power of the sword. Many, like Nicodemus, find it difficult to think in any other terms except those of the physical and material aspects of life. We can explain the phenomena of nature to which Jesus called Nicodemus' attention as people in that day could not, but we are still as blind and deaf to the urgency of the spiritual. We can split an atom, but we cannot unite a split world. We listen with pathetic avidity to the latest word from our favorite news commentator or columnist, but will not, like Hezekiah, ask, "Is there any word from the Lord?" [3]

Yet this is the very question men need to ask, for where else can they turn to find an authority that is constant, but not static; dependable, but not dominating; absolute, but allowing freedom for creativity and growth? Where else can they find an authority on which they can depend as a guide for their lives as surely as a navigator depends upon the north magnetic pole to guide him through uncharted seas? For men need a star that can guide them through the darkness of these perilous times and through life's perplexing problems.

The tragedy is, that in their eagerness to find an answer to the quest for meaning and stability in life, millions are not careful to differentiate between authority and authoritarianism; between that which rests on truth and that which rests on mere dogmatism. Therefore, they give their loyalty to that which restricts, rather than reinforces, their lives and their liberties. Thus we see in the world the rise of totalitarian movements in which people surrender even their precious freedom to seek and declare the truth in exchange for what seems to offer them a greater measure of security and support. Having lost the view of an eternal order of truth and love in which each individual has significance as an immortal soul, many are willing to settle for whatever security they can get in this world and, if hungry enough, will, as someone has put it, put four sandwiches ahead of the four freedoms.

In seeking God's answer to man's basic problems and needs, Protestant Christianity has always contended that our basic authority, both for faith and conduct, is the Bible; that it, as no other source, speaks God's authoritative word to men. The Bible, Protestant Christianity points out, is made up of abiding truths, the validity of which has been tested and tried by long centuries of experience. Men did not invent these truths any more than they invented the sunrise. They experienced them, and in moments of deep insight and understanding, as some new phase of God's truth dawned or, in some cases, flashed upon them, they wrote down what they had perceived to the glory of God and the enlightenment of men. The fact that we still live under the judgments of the Bible's teachings after centuries of time and testing, and that they still offer us our greatest guidance and hope, is convincing evidence of the validity of the Bible and of the inspiration under which its insights were received and written down.

The Bible, however, is not so much a dissertation about life as an *interpretation of life*. It deals primarily with events and their meaning—first, events in the life of Israel —and leads up to what it presents as the supreme event in all history—the coming of Jesus into the life of the World. In writing the Bible, men did not begin with ideas and then think up situations to illustrate them. They began with experiences in which they felt they had been confronted by the Lord himself, and, under the inspiration of that encounter, they set out, as has so often been said, to interpret history as "His story."

When seen through eyes of faith, the Bible is not so much a record of man's quest for God—indeed, men, for the most part, have been distressingly indifferent to any real quest for God—but of God's quest for man. Beginning with the revelation of himself and his purposes through the law and the prophets, "His story" culminates with the full revelation of his character and love in the person and work of Jesus Christ.

That is why even the Bible itself is, in great measure, a closed book apart from Jesus. For while it is true that Jesus' earthly life cannot be understood apart from his Hebraic background, it is equally true that the teachings of the Old Testament take on their greatest meaning when considered in the light of the life and teachings of Jesus. Jesus once said, "Search the scriptures; for in them ye think ye have eternal life: and they are they which testify of me." [4] Unless the spirit and purposes of him who loved men and gave himself for them stand revealed on its pages, what does it profit us to read the Bible?

How little, for example, we would understand Isaiah's great concept of the "Suffering Servant" role as portrayed in the fifty-third chapter of his book if we did not see its prophetic insights fulfilled in the life and death of Jesus. How limited would be our understanding of Paul's inspired utterance on love in the familiar thirteenth chapter of 1 Corinthians if we did not see such love mirrored in the life and ministry of Jesus. Jesus is the key that unlocks the Scriptures. He brings to light what God is trying to say to us through the Bible. We understand toward what the prophets were reaching because we know him.

Without a knowledge of Jesus, we read the Bible through a glass darkly. The Bible takes on its supreme significance because it brings us face to face with Jesus: the Old Testament because it points toward him; the New Testament because it presents and interprets him. Apart from Jesus, the Bible is good advice. With him at the center, it becomes good news.

Of course, we need help in interpreting Jesus' message and meaning for our lives today in the light of present-day situations and needs. Jesus said we would. In fact, he once promised just such continuing guidance and help. "When he, the Spirit of truth, is come," he said, "he will guide you into all truth." [5] Only as we seek the aid of God's Holy Spirit through personal commitment and prayer, and through the enriching, meaningful fellowship of the Christian church can we hope fully to know God's guidance and will for our lives today. But we can never know God's love and will apart from Jesus' revelation of them.

Here, then, are the twin rails that make up the track of revelation on which we can run a guided life: a knowledge of the historic revelation of God's love and will in the life and work of Jesus, plus an inner consciousness of God's guidance as we seek the companionship of his Holy Spirit. We must have both. We must, through prayer, meditation, and commitment, seek to know God's will for our lives today. But we must also, through a knowledge of the Bible, check our sense of guidance against an understanding of the character and will of God as revealed through the insights of the prophets, and supremely through the person and work of Jesus; for without that we would have no objective standard by which to judge our inner experience of God's guidance. We might, therefore, be misled as to what we would conceive to be God's will for our lives and times.

In fact, Jesus points to an extreme example of this very possibility. In the chapter in which we read of his promise of the Comforter, he warns the disciples of the day when he who persecutes them to the death "will think that he doeth God's service." [6] By failing to consider their actions in the light of Jesus and his love, men would have no proper criterion by which to judge their conduct, and would therefore miss the cue as to what constitutes the divine purpose for their lives. But by accepting God's revelation of himself in Jesus, plus the direct revelation of himself to the heart of the sensitive seeker after truth, one has a twofold guide that can lead him into a further knowledge of the truth and of God's will for his life.

That Jesus was able, in view of his earthly circumstances, to bring the revelation he did is still the miracle of the ages. In a country no larger than the state of Maryland, with no press or radio to publicize his movements, he walked into history. He was in the public eye no more than three years at most. He resorted to no tricks to attract public attention. On the contrary, he frequently discouraged his friends from publicizing his activities lest it attract the wrong kind of a following. Comparatively few people followed him. The religious leaders of his day repudiated him, and finally were responsible for having him put to death. He met a criminal's death between two thieves while still in his early thirties, and was buried in a borrowed tomb.

These facts are generally well-known. And yet no person in all history has left in his wake such an influence for truth and righteousness as Jesus has. For his followers believe that the grave did not hold him; that he is alive today to lead men by his Spirit. Thus, he has continued to cut an ever-widening swathe in history, so that today more people than ever before claim him both as the Lord of history and of their lives. Only the wilfully stubborn would refuse to recognize his influence in and on history. To millions he is the Christ, the Son of the living God.

Wherever he went, he taught. He taught in the synagogues and on the mountainsides. He taught by the seashore. The homes of his friends became his classrooms. Much of what he said was not recorded. Much of what remains to us has been colored by the interpretation of his hearers and translators. But look at his words in the light of his life, and his teachings make an unmistakable impression, the essential lines of which stand out all the more clearly because they stand at such sharp variance with most of the accepted standards and practices of the world.

Today, one frequently hears the cry, "Back to God." Men, we are told, must get back to God, or civilization will perish. But it makes all the difference in the world the kind of a God to whom people believe they must return. No God of our own making or conception can save us. Only the God whose power and purposes have been indicated in history and whose nature had been supremely revealed in Jesus can do that. For Jesus came to reveal, in terms that men could understand, the true and full nature of God. To know God fully, therefore, we must know Jesus. And to know Jesus, we must know something about his teachings, since no one can know another without knowing something of his thoughts and ideals.

Let it be said at once, however, that Jesus was more than just a teacher. He came not merely to teach the way of life, but to reveal it. He did not say, "I *know* the way, the truth, and the life," but, "I *am* the way, the truth, and the life." [7] To know him, he said, is to know the Father. His primary purpose was not just to teach new truths about God, but to reveal God's love in a way that would bring men into a new and transforming relationship with God through knowing him.

He did not come, for example, just to outline a new set of virtues or to announce the golden rule. Many of the virtues we call Christian today were stressed long before the Christian era. The Greeks laid great stress on the cardinal virtues: prudence, justice, temperance, and fortitude. Philo likened them to four rivers that flow from the mind of God. [8] But virtues are humanly achievable. In order to be rescued from sin, mankind needs that which must be divinely given. If the preaching of virtues could have saved the world, Jesus need not have come.

That is not to say that Jesus did not teach certain virtues, or that he did not, by his living of them, put new content into their meaning. He did both. Many of his parables were told to stress the importance of some particular virtue or discipline. In the parable of the unjust steward, for example, he teaches the value of foresight.[9] In the parable of the importunate widow, he teaches persistence in prayer.[10] "It is quite clear," writes Dr. A. J. Gossip, "that sincerity is one of our Lord's favorite virtues; and, in his eyes, the foundation of everything."[11] But Jesus knew that the mere teaching of virtues is not enough. He came not merely to tell us how to live, but how, through faith in God, to find life, so we may experience life's truest and most satisfying values and face even eternity itself with confidence and hope.

Let us put it this way. Jesus came not merely to lead men upward in their quest for God, but to bring God down to men. In a stimulating little book, Dr. Shirley Jackson Case is quoted as saying there are two kinds of religion: the religion of achievement and the religion of rescue.[12] The religion of achievement urges men to achieve a knowledge of God and acceptance with God by climbing up the double ladder of reason and obedience to his laws. In the religion of rescue, God comes down the ladder of revelation to men. Climbing up to God is usually defined as meaning obedience to certain well-defined religious and ethical laws. It is as if religion said to us, "If, by trying hard enough, you manage to obey certain rites and regulations, you may, after a while, become good enough that even God can love you."

But what kind of a hope is that to a person who is wrestling with his doubts and trying to climb out of his sins? Of course, reason has its place, but man, by reason alone, cannot hope to know God. God is infinite; man is finite. The more he tries by mental searching to find out God, the more he realizes his ladder is short, and the heavens are high. Nor can one climb out of his sins. The more he tries, the more he becomes conscious of the weight of the carnal nature that holds him back. What he needs is enlightenment from beyond himself and the assurance of forgiveness for his sins; for man, by his own efforts, can never climb high enough fully to know or to merit God's love. Dr. Oscar Blackwelder, who for many years ministered in a church near the United States Supreme Court building, is fond of pointing out that the marble of which the Supreme Court building is constructed is so white that under the summer sun it fairly blinds one to look at it, but when it snows, the building looks gray. Our whiteness is a dismal gray compared to the purity and perfection of God.

Moreover, love cannot be earned; it must be given, or it is not love. A parent does not love his child just because the child behaves, but because it is his child. Naturally, he wants the child to obey, but if he is a true parent, he continues to love the child even when he is disobedient. Fortunately, we do not have to wait until we understand or deserve God's mercy in order to receive it; for Christianity—which is a religion of rescue—says that God loves us, not because we deserve his love, but because we are his children and it is his nature to love. Thus Paul could write that "God commendeth his love toward us, in that, *while we were yet sinners*, Christ died for us." [13]

This is the very heart of the gospel. Perhaps it can be illustrated this way. Frequently it happens that a fashionable church that has been a leading church in a downtown community finds itself in a rapidly deteriorating neighborhood. If it seeks to adapt its program so as to minister to the needs of the children in the changing community, some of the members (a majority of whom have moved to the more beautiful suburbs) are apt to complain, "We wouldn't mind those children coming around the church if they were not so destructive."

Such an attitude is understandable. After all, church furniture costs money, and ought to be respected. But if the children, many of whom come from anything but a Christian home, have to wait until they are perfect little gentle-

men and ladies before they are allowed to enter the church
and use its facilities, they are lost already. Their only hope
is for someone to love them as they are for the sake of
what they may become with the right kind of understanding and guidance. And that, after all, is the way God loves
us. For Christianity says that, in Christ, God came down
to show weak, sinful humans that he loves them, not because they deserve his love, but because it is his nature to
love. Where we could not lift ourselves, he came to lift
us up. What we could not attain by our own efforts, he
came to give us as a gift that we, through the gift of his
love, might attain the stature of sons of God.

That does not mean that our role is merely a passive one.
Obviously, it involves both the willingness and the capacity on our part to respond. In Christ, God has amply revealed that his "hand is not shortened, that it cannot
save," [14] but we, through faith and commitment, must
reach out to grasp his outstretched hand.

A church convention chose as its theme, "The Magnetic
Christ." The choice was a good one. Jesus once said, "And
I, if I be lifted up from the earth, will draw all men unto
me." [15] But a magnet cannot draw that which does not have
within itself the capacity to respond. It cannot, for example, pick up a piece of string. But let it be moved toward a
steel needle, and the needle itself will be seen to respond
to the pull of the magnet. Without the existence of lines
of magnetic force, a ship's compass would be a useless in-
strument. But by responding to the pull of such magnetic
lines, the compass enables the captain to steer his ship safely
into harbor through the darkest night. Without the reality
of God's love as revealed in Christ and his cross, our efforts to achieve the good life would be a sad mockery, but
with that assurance we can give ourselves to a life of faith
and love, knowing that our "labour is not in vain in the
Lord." [16]

Jesus, then, came not just to teach us, but to save us; not just to add to our knowledge of God, but to bring us into a new and saving relationship to him.

Indeed, if Jesus is to save us, he has to be more than a teacher, since education alone can never save us. We stand in inexpressible gratitude for all education has done, and is doing, for us and our world. Without it, we would grow up to be little more than savages. For education passes on from one generation to the next the vast amount ot knowledge and wisdom that have been accumulated by the human race. Surely, the teacher is one of the most valuable persons in the community.

We know, however, that education is limited in what it can do for the human spirit. It cannot heal a broken heart or cleanse a guilty one. It cannot provide men with an eternal hope. At best, it can provide civilization with a veneer of culture; and in the light of two world wars and their aftermath, we have seen how thin that veneer of civilization can be. Education does not meet man's basic needs because it does not get at the basic problem of man's sinfulness. An educated sinner is still a sinner. Indeed, he may be more fiendishly clever than he was before. "The only thing worse than a devil," says Dr. George A. Buttrick, "is an educated devil." [17]

Thus education, in and of itself, does not insure a finer person or a better world. Men cannot live without education and remain civilized, but neither can they live by education alone. Men need friendship that can match their loneliness, a sense of purpose that can give direction and meaning to this life, and a hope for the life to come. That is one reason, at least, why the author of Ecclesiastes, before finding a satisfying purpose for life, could write, "I gave my heart to know wisdom, and . . . I perceived that . . . in much wisdom is grief: and he that increaseth knowledge increaseth sorrow." [18] The world is discovering

the truth of that statement now that men know enough to
know how to create the threat of atomic destruction.
Sometimes the increasing of knowledge can provide us
with new ways of being lost.

Let us go one step further and admit that in his teachings Jesus set up unattainable goals.[19] That is part of the
challenge of them. Who wants only goals he can attain?
Jesus did not limit himself to stating what he felt men could
achieve, but what God desires and expects. Being perfect
himself, God can be satisfied with nothing less than perfection. That is why our hope depends upon his goodness
rather than on our own. If being a Christian means living
up to all the teachings of Jesus, who, then, can be a Christian? But if being a Christian means putting our trust in
Christ, then by his indwelling Spirit he enables us to become, not perfect, but sons of God, whose lives are filled
with a sense of the glory and goodness of God, and whose
supreme desire, in spite of our weaknesses and shortcomings, is to do the will of God.

In fact, we must trust Jesus before we can begin to live
out his teachings. As Dr. Charles A. Ellwood reminds us,
"The imitation of Christ, as he himself emphasized, requires, as it were, a spiritual rebirth—a vision of a way of
life totally different from that of natural man." [20] It is as
foolish to expect a person who has not come to know and
love Jesus to live out the teachings of the Sermon on the
Mount as it would be to expect two persons who are not
in love with each other to build an ideal home together.
It is only as we surrender our will to Christ that we begin
to experience the transformation of life and attitudes that
make it possible to begin to live out his teachings.

Nevertheless, having said all this, Jesus was a teacher.
He was recognized as such by his contemporaries. Indeed,
they acclaimed him to be a very great and unusual one.
"We know that thou art a teacher come from God," [21] said

Nicodemus, thereby paying him a great, if perhaps a grudging, compliment. "The common people," Mark tells us, "heard him gladly," [22] and Matthew adds, "The people were astonished at his doctrine: for he taught them as one having authority, and not as the scribes." [23] Luke tells us, "His word was with power." [24] When the temple guards were sent to arrest him, they came back empty-handed, giving as their reason, "Never man spake like this man." [25] When asked if they also would desert him, Peter, speaking for the disciples, answered, "Lord, to whom shall we go? thou hast the words of eternal life." [26]

Moreover, Jesus himself set great store by his teachings. "Why call ye me, Lord, Lord," he demanded, "and do not the things which I say?" [27] And again he said, "Whosoever heareth these sayings of mine, and doeth them, I will liken him unto a wise man, which built his house upon a rock: . . . And every one that heareth these sayings of mine, and doeth them not, shall be likened unto a foolish man, which built his house upon the sand." [28]

Jesus expected his teachings to be taken seriously. The fact that the Apostles' Creed jumps from the birth of Jesus to his trial before Pilate, with no reference to his intervening ministry and teachings, is surely a regrettable omission. His teachings are not mere accessories to be taken or left at will. They constitute an integral part of his revelation of God, and as such are guideposts that indicate the way of life. Civilization ignores these guideposts to its own peril; for, to know Jesus, to know something of his deep insights into the nature of God and man, is to have the highest concept of the meaning and purpose for life this world can know. Such an understanding of the master Teacher gives us guideposts that point the way to victory over sin and despair.

II.

HOW HE TAUGHT

As one enters the Bliss Electrical School in Takomah Park, Maryland, he is confronted by two statements that hang on the wall, each containing a reference to education. The first sign reads, "Education is the armour of organized knowledge against the natural enemies of human happiness, and everyone should have its protection be the cost what it may." The second sign reads, "Education is the process of acquiring a reverence for accuracy and a respect for ideals." Both signs emphasize the importance of education. Ideas are transmitted, lives changed, civilizations influenced by great teaching.

It is no wonder, then, that Jesus gave so much of his time to teaching as he sought to bring people into a new awareness and understanding of God. This fact is highly significant, for it reveals much about his fundamental approach to people and his methods of imparting his matchless truths to their minds and hearts. Of course, he often preached to great multitudes of people—sometimes to thousands. For the most part, however, he seems to have spent much of his time dealing with individuals and small groups. By studying his teaching methods, we can learn much about the right way to approach people and try to impart to them the basic concepts of the Christian way of life.

This is important, because today we live in a world of clashing ideologies. The ideology of freedom, of free men

16

in a free society, is being challenged by an ideology of regimentation and coercion. The ideology of understanding and good will is confronted by an ideology of hate and distrust. The ideology of religious faith and values is loudly challenged by an ideology of materialism and economic determinism. Marxian communism today stands condemned by free minds, not only for what it teaches but for how it teaches it. It resorts to force, not facts, to establish its tenets. It seeks to impose an enforced collectivism rather than to invite and inspire voluntary co-operation. All individuals and facts are made to fit the Procrustean bed of its political purposes and program.

Jesus, on the other hand, merits the attention and respect of every honest seeker after truth, not only for what he taught but for the way he taught it. He set the pattern for all to follow who wish to seek and to share truth. His symbol is a cross, not a club. He chose the way of the teacher, not the tyrant, as he set out to open men's eyes to eternal truth and to open their hearts to God's abiding love. In a world where whole populations are being browbeaten and tortured in a process of indoctrination known as "brainwashing," and where the very word "propaganda" has come to have an ominous ring, we do well to study Jesus' teaching methods and his approach to people.

How little the disciples must have realized, as they sat listening to the words of Jesus, what an incomparable privilege they were enjoying. Not only were they hearing the actual sound of Jesus' voice; not only could they look into his face and watch his eloquent gestures as he spoke, but in their hearing were being unfolded the most significant teachings the world has ever known. Here was wisdom for which the world had been waiting. Here was spiritual insight which, if followed, could lead men out of the darkness of ignorance and fear into the light of a new day. Here were teachings that, more than any other, have challenged the consciences of men and opened their eyes to abiding values and eternal truth.

How impoverished the world would be without the teachings of Jesus! Brief as they are—and unquestionably we have only a mere fraction of what he said—they constitute the profoundest wisdom as to the nature of God and man this world has ever known. There are those, of course, who dismiss them as the mouthings of an impractical visionary. Even among those who profess to believe in his teachings, they are more quoted than followed. But wherever they have been tried, even on a limited scale, life has been lifted to new levels of freedom and joy, men's eyes have been opened to a new scale of values, and life has taken on new meaning and direction. Even those who do not accept Jesus as Lord and Saviour are impressed by the loftiness of his teachings, and long wistfully for the time when men will begin to follow them.

The charge is often made that Jesus said nothing that has not been said before. "We have been told over and over again," writes Dr. W. A. Smart, "that practically all the teachings of Jesus can be duplicated in the teachings of the rabbis." "But," he adds significantly, "the rabbis did not set the world aflame." [1] The teachings of Jesus were not the dull repetitions of old authorities. He spoke with authority. His teachings were presented with such assurance and insight that men marveled at the authority with which he spoke. His words were like new wine. What he had to say about God and his relationship to men was so vital and transforming that it could not be contained in old concepts and patterns. Old forms of provincialism and pride were cracked open, permitting new streams of love and joy to flow to mankind.

Moreover, it can also be said that never has spiritual truth been understood and stated so clearly. Never have such profound thoughts been expressed so simply or with such luminous clarity. Never have words taken on such a rich and significant meaning as when seen through the spectrum of his life and ministry. His own life, as he himself suggested, was the best attestation of the validity of his doctrine.[2]

Furthermore, there was a new sense of certainty in all he said. No other teacher has ever gone so far in declaring the love and purposes of God. Certainly, none has ever gone so far in claiming to know the true nature of God. Either his claims were true or they were a delusion. But surely a false delusion could never have produced such a glorious life or such marvelous consequences in history. Jesus' life bathed his teachings in light. His death was his most cogent argument for the love and concern of God. His resurrection and the ongoing life of the church have validated his message. Truly he was a teacher come from God.

But how did Jesus teach? How did he impart his unparalleled insights into life's deepest meanings so that even his humblest followers could understand and remember his teachings? This, too, is important to know if we would share his message with the world. It is not enough to have something to say. One must know how to say it with clarity and persuasiveness. Since Jesus did not reduce his teachings to writing; since he depended on the memories of his hearers to perpetuate his thoughts and words, it becomes all the more important to know how Jesus sought to impress his undying truths on the minds and hearts of his hearers. How, then, did Jesus present the truths that, more than any other, have given men insight into the very heart and mind of God and a new understanding of the true meaning of existence?

Obviously, Jesus' teachings cannot be considered apart from his life. What he said took on new significance because of what he was and did. There is a revealing comment in Luke's account of the resurrection. When the disciples realized in their own experience the fulfilment of Jesus' promise that he would rise again, then, Luke tells us, "they remembered his words." [3] Apart from his crucifixion and resurrection, certain teachings of Jesus would have had no meaning for them and would have been quickly forgotten. But in the light of what happened in the life of Jesus, his words were recalled and burned forever into their memories. They remembered the words of Jesus because of the experiences that gave them import. Nevertheless, apart from the obvious connection between his words and his life, Jesus' approach to people is worthy of our most careful consideration. For, whether his audience was one or many, certain principles seemed to guide his methods; principles that must be made a part of all effective efforts to teach and to create happy human relationships.

To begin with, Jesus was always conscious of the personal worth and needs of every person to whom he spoke. Someone has suggested there are four rules of salesmanship a good teacher should seek to follow. First, he must capture the attention of those with whom he would share his ideas. Second, he must clearly state his purpose—what it is he is trying to say. Third, he must know how to present his facts, arguments, and illustrations so as to be convincing. Finally, he must appeal for a decision.

In all these respects, Jesus was a master teacher. He knew how, without having to resort to sensationalism, to attract and hold the attention of his hearers. He was unsurpassed in his ability to present and illustrate truth. Being the wise teacher he was, he did not fail to state his purpose. On frequent occasions he stated the goal of his mission so men would know why he felt he had come and what he hoped to accomplish. He always appealed for decision and commitment.

We are not for one moment, however, trying to cast Jesus in the role of a supersalesman. He was not a salesman, but a Saviour. His purpose was not to "sell" ideas, but to save people by winning them to a total response to his total gospel of love and life. He did not try to use people as a means toward an end, but made their fulfilment and redemption the end toward which he lived and died. His was no "big-jug-little-mug" method of teaching in which the teacher conceives his task to be that of pouring his superior fund of knowledge into the less-filled minds of his hearers. Jesus was much too conscious of his hearers as persons for that. Of course, there were certain ideas with which he had to deal, but his primary effort was not just to fill men's minds with new thoughts about God, but to transform their hopes and lives by bringing them into a new relationship with God. He thought of men not as receptacles for his truth, but as responders to his way of life. His purpose was not to impose knowledge, but to enlist discipleship; not to impress with learning, but to invite trust and devotion; not just to educate, but to emancipate and to help men, through faith in him, to find the "power to become the sons of God," [4] so that, enjoying true fellowship with God, they might reflect more of his truth and his love.

More important than any methods Jesus may have used were his motives; and certainly one of his most compelling motives was his genuine love and concern for people. He was concerned about what happened to people whose problems and needs he knew so well through intimate contact. The very fact that he had to walk from place to place gave him a tremendous advantage in meeting and dealing with people—an advantage that we who speed by in our high-powered cars do not have, and must depend upon Gallup polls and news analysts to find out what the people are thinking. No persons were beneath his notice. That the poor should have the gospel preached to them was as important to him as that the blind should be made to see and the lame to walk.

Watching him in the presence of the multitudes, Matthew could say, "When he saw the multitudes, he was moved with compassion on them." [5] His compassion often opened the way for his teaching. Men often listened to his words because they felt he was genuinely interested in them and in their problems. He was concerned about the plight of publicans and sinners. He was concerned about the poor and the hungry. He was concerned because people "fainted, and were scattered abroad, as sheep having no shepherd." [6] He was concerned because they needed a physician who could minister to their total needs. To him, every individual was equally the object of God's love and concern. Always, therefore, in his approach to people, he considered them as persons, each deserving his equal candor and love.

As one reads the teachings of Jesus, it is obvious that he built upon the Holy Scriptures of his people. They were his spiritual food and drink. At the outset of his public ministry, he could strengthen his unfaltering purpose and resistance to temptation by drawing upon the inspiration and insights of the Word. If his adversaries could argue from the Scriptures, he could do so even more. His repeated references to the Old Testament show both his utter familiarity with its message and his thorough grasp of its meaning. As he hung upon the cross, appropriate words from the sacred Book came naturally to his lips. Always, when he needed it, he could call to mind the right passage. Also, in his use of the Scriptures, he showed that he had penetrated more deeply into their essential meaning than those who boasted a more scholarly knowledge of the sacred writings.

"It is accepted," writes W. M. Grant, "that our Lord

went to the Old Testament for the essence of his teachings. It was to the Old Testament," he continues, "that he went for his doctrine of God and man; he found in the spiritual teaching of the prophets a mirror of his mission, and he claimed that he had come to fulfil the Scriptures. In a wide range of quotation, allusion, and echo he gathered the wealth of the Book into his speech, and appealed to the religious experience of the Hebrew Cloud of Witnesses for the illustration and confirmation of his message." [7]

But Jesus went deeper. He probed to the very heart of man and revealed the very heart of God. He dared at times to take issue with the ancient writings. "It was said by them of old time . . . but I say unto you." The law forbade certain breaches of conduct, but Jesus probed beneath the overt expressions of sin to expose their festering sources: the hatreds and pride, the wicked imaginations, the contempt for personality, the selfish attitudes and longings from which such conduct springs. He went behind the letter of the law to reveal its purpose, and made his court of final appeal, not the law of Moses, but his own understanding of the redemptive love and will of God. In fact, he openly declared himself to be not merely an interpreter of the Scriptures, but the One in whom they were to be perfectly realized. Even after his resurrection, we read concerning him that "beginning at Moses and all the prophets, he expounded unto them in all the scriptures the things concerning himself." [8]

Jesus' use of the Scriptures is revealed in his controversies with his adversaries. When they sought to distort his truth and reject his claims, he frequently brought them up short and backed up his own contentions by calling to his support some passage of Scripture they could neither refute nor deny. When questioned about the "greatest commandment," he showed how even the law itself points to love, both for God and man, as the supreme requirement.

When the Sadducees sought to caricature the idea of immortality, he upbraided them for superimposing their own crude concepts of the flesh on what the Scriptures so patently reveal to be the kingdom of the Spirit. When righteous indignation drove him to cleanse the Temple, he lashed its desecraters, not with a rope, but with the plain teachings of the Scriptures concerning God's house of prayer.

On another occasion, when he entered Jerusalem to make one last bid for the support of the leaders of his people, the Scriptures dictated the manner of his entrance. Against the haunting and horrible memory of conquerors who had typified their might and arrogance by haughtily riding into Jerusalem astride a prancing steed of war, Zachariah had envisioned the coming of a new kind of leader who would express his humility and willingness to serve the people by choosing instead a humble beast of burden.[9] Jesus knew this prophecy. Moreover, he knew that the people knew it. Whether it was in his mind at the time of his triumphal entry into Jerusalem—and we can well believe it was—the people seem to have made the connection, for when they saw him coming seated on a borrowed donkey, they hailed him as "he that cometh in the name of the Lord." [10]

Thus, the Scriptures became Jesus' rod of defense against his enemies. More important, God's Word served as his point of contact with the people as he sought repeatedly to show them that he had come, not to destroy, but to fulfil the law and the prophets.

One of the reasons the common people heard him gladly was that he spoke to them in language they could understand. Of course, it was the content of his message rather than the method of its presentation that attracted and held them. Nevertheless, he put his eternal truths into pictures and stories they could not forget. No other teacher in all history has been able to use such apt illustrations as he.

Paul, with all his brilliance, was clumsy by comparison in his use of illustrations.

Jesus knew the mental sluggishness of many with whom he had to deal. Again and again he had to spell out his meaning to those who misunderstood even the plainest of his teachings. Thus he clothed many of his teachings in pictures that made an indelible impression upon them. He knew the recall value of a story. Long after it has forgotten his arguments, a congregation will remember a preacher's illustrations. "Stories," said that gifted teller of stories, William L. Stidger, "are windows in the dark tower of a sermon to let in more light." [11] And John Henry Jowett, the great Scotch preacher, used to say, "A story often catches him whom a sermon misses." [12] Jesus' parables have been called his "chief and most persuasive preaching method." [13] Dr. Charles Francis McKoy points out that in Jesus' teachings there are "no classical allusions to events in the history of Rome or Greece; few lessons drawn from any of the events of extra-Biblical history; and no quotations from the poets and philosophers of pagan civilization." [14] Instead, he illustrated his messages with the commonplace things of everyday life with which even the humblest in his audiences were familiar.

What shepherd, for example, ever forgot his simple, but telling, references to sheep? What planter would fail to be intrigued by his parable of the sower, or what housewife fail to remember his illustration of the leaven? The grotesque picture of a man whose own vision was blinded by an entire plank foolishly fumbling to remove a mere speck of sawdust from another's eye must have moved Jesus' hearers to laughter; but it must also have focused their attention on their own sins and shortcomings more than any amount of learned discussion of the problem of conscience could have done.

We must not, of course, make the mistake of underesti-

mating the intellectual grasp of Jesus' teachings because of
the simplicity of his illustrations. The Pharisees were not
apt to make that error after matching wits with him on
several occasions and always coming off second best. The
modern world tends to underestimate the sheer intellectual
stature of Jesus. It fails to agree with Dr. V. G. Simko-
vitch, who says, "To me personally, it seems childish not
to see in Christ's teachings an overwhelming intellectual
system," and again, "In Christ the one thing that stands out
monumentally is his intellectual grandeur." [15]

While Jesus' intellectual grandeur is but one facet of his
marvelous life, we do need to be reminded of the scope
and depth of his intellectual understanding. The teachings
of Jesus are simple, but not superficial. They plumb the
greatest depths. The humblest mind can grasp their essential meaning, but the most scholarly stand in awe before
their profundity. The world cannot shrug off the teachings
of Jesus as if they did not matter. They get to the very
heart of man's predicament and give God's answer to that
predicament. They cannot be ignored or rejected with im-
punity.

But Jesus not only used the spoken word, he taught by
psychological suggestion and visible symbol. Long before
psychology had been formulated as a science for studying
human behavior, he followed its valid principles and pio-
neered in its methods. When Simon revealed his depth of
spiritual insight by recognizing the deeper significance of
Jesus and his mission, Jesus rewarded him by calling him
Peter, meaning "a rock," thereby giving his gifted, but
sometimes unstable, disciple something to live up to all the
rest of his life. Whatever he may have meant theologically,
psychologically Jesus challenged Simon to a steadfast discipleship that would have real significance, not only for
Simon, but for the life of the early church as well.

Or consider the teaching value of the Lord's Supper.

When Jesus would give his disciples a memorial of his death, he used symbols they would never forget. To men familiar with the symbolism of the Passover meal by which they were reminded of Israel's liberation from Egypt and of their solidarity as a people, Jesus took bread and the cup and made them reminders of his own death and the part it was to play in their larger liberation from bondage to sin, as well as the part their own fellowship was to play as a continuing body on the earth.

Here again Jesus showed his genius as a teacher, for, again, whatever other significance the Lord's Supper is intended to have (and its significance far transcends that of a mere reminder [16]) here was, and is, teaching at its best. What Jesus said to the disciples, they might tend to forget unless it were associated with some visible symbol to fix it in their minds; some visible means to fix and retain it in their consciousness. So he took bread and broke it, saying, "This is my body, which is broken for you," [17] and he bade them eat. He took the cup saying, "This is my blood of the new testament, which is shed for many for the remission of sins," and he bade them drink.

Jesus could not have chosen more effective or eloquent symbols, for men everywhere eat and drink. Everywhere, therefore, men have at their disposal the visible means whereby they may be reminded of his broken body and shed blood. Thus by the simple observance of this memorial meal, believers can be reminded more forcibly than by volumes of words of the real meaning of his death, the wonder of his love, and of the glorious hope through his resurrection, of the mystery of his presence. Such a fellowship of faith binds them together in the church, which is his body in the world today.

But Jesus did not limit his teaching to the spoken word and visible symbol. One of the most effective ways he taught his followers was to lead them into experiences where they would learn for themselves. People learn by doing. The best way to verify truth is to put it to the test. The best way to learn to pray is to pray. The best way to learn the power of love is to love. Jesus himself stated this principle of learning when he said, "If any man will do his will, he shall learn of the doctrine, whether it be of God, or whether I speak of myself." [18] Thus he invited men to try his way of life and let the results speak for themselves.

One cannot teach swimming in a classroom. It must be learned in water where, under proper coaching, one learns to keep his body afloat. Jesus did not merely warn his followers of the perils of discipleship, he sent them out, two by two, into a world where he told them they would be as "lambs among wolves." [19] To teach them to rely on spiritual rather than material resources, he told them to carry "neither purse, nor scrip, nor shoes." [20] When they returned, he carefully questioned them about their experiences. When they replied, "Even the devils are subject unto us through thy name," he "rejoiced in spirit," [21] knowing that though hardships were ahead of them, they had learned from actual experience God's power to sustain those who act through faith in him.

Jesus used the right order when he said, "I am the way, the truth, and the life." [22] Men learn the truth by walking the way. Experience precedes doctrine. Men experienced Christ before they formulated doctrines about him. We do not experience the joys of the Christian life by defining it, but by living it. Sometimes we try to reverse the order. We tend to put creed before commitment. Jesus put discipleship before doctrine. Not that doctrine is unimportant. After all, he did ask the disciples, "Whom say ye that I am?" But first he said, "Follow me." They came to the realization of his significance as a Person by walking the path along which he led them.

Indeed, the doctrine would have been incomprehensible

without the experience. Let a person experience the miracle of the new birth, and the miracle of the incarnation
becomes credible. To men who challenged him about his
belief in the miracle at Cana, where Jesus is said to have
turned water into wine, a humble Welch miner replied, "In
my home, he turned whisky into furniture." There was the
basis for his belief. He could believe what Jesus had done
in Cana because of what he had done in the miner's own
home, where he had changed the miner from a drunkard
into a sober, family-supporting husband and father.

Jesus still reserves some of his deepest insights for those
who will enter the arena of action with him. Too much religion in these days is spectator religion. Too many people
want inspiration without participation. Except when they
want something of God or the church, many, without
Job's provocation, cry out with him, "Let me alone." [23] It
is always easier to watch from the sidelines than to play the
game, but that is not how scores are made, either on the
playing field or in the Christian life. It is easier to discuss
religion than to practice it, but it is in the very exercise of
faith that people find its true value. Jesus still tries to teach
us by calling us into a life of discipleship, knowing that
faith is proved by the living of it. If one never took a step
by faith, he would never know if his faith were valid. It is
by living his faith that one becomes convinced of its validity and vitality.

Perhaps no profession in all the world requires greater
patience than that of teaching. Here again Jesus showed his
genius as a teacher. He took the disciples where they were
and led them on to new truth. He met people at the point
of their deepest need. He was as willing to take time for one
seeking sinner as for the multitudes. He did not deal in
mere generalities, but began with life situations in which
his followers found themselves and tried to show them
what his way of life required of them in such a context. To

men who followed the occupation of fishing, he challenged
their interest in his kingdom by promising to make them
fishers of men. To people forced to carry a Roman's burden a mile, he urged them to take the spiritual initiative by
carrying it two. To disciples who argued over preferred
status in his new kingdom, he took a child and set him in
their midst, declaring that unless they achieved something
of the guileless faith and sense of dependence of a child,
they could not even enter the kingdom of the Spirit. As a
teacher, Jesus recognized the importance of children, so
that when the disciples expressed typical adult irritation
toward them, Jesus rebuked them in no uncertain terms,
saying, "of such is the kingdom of heaven." [24] A poor
widow giving an offering with which she could ill-afford
to part provided him with the background for one of his
most telling observations on the test of one's stewardship
in the sight of God.

To those who believed in an old covenant between God
and the nation, he proclaimed a new covenant between
God and the individual believer. To those who thought of
Israel as the vineyard of the Lord,[25] he declared himself to
be "the true vine," and his followers "the branches." [26] To
those familiar with the phrase, "the yoke of the law," [27]
and who bore the galling yoke of innumerable regulations
and prohibitions imposed upon them by stern, unyielding
legalists, Jesus said, "Take my yoke upon you, and learn of
me: for I am meek and lowly in heart: and ye shall find
rest unto your souls." [28] Like the master teacher he was,
he found out what his disciples were thinking by asking
them questions: "Whom do men say that I . . . am?"
Then with perfect timing, "Whom say ye that I am?" [29] He
did not give them ready-made answers to their questions,
but helped them to find the right answers for themselves.

He did not take his pupils faster than they could go. It
was inconceivable to the Jews of his day that the Messiah

should have to suffer and die, and so he seems to have guarded against the use of that term, preferring instead the simpler, more general, title, "Son of man." Since the term, "son of David," had such political connotations in the minds of his hearers, he sought to put new content into its meaning before letting his disciples use it. As a wise teacher, he knew that students who are still studying the multiplication tables are not yet ready for algebra. Even at the end, he had to say to them, "I have yet many things to say unto you, but ye cannot bear them now." [30]

Above all else, however, Jesus taught by precept and example. When his disciples asked him, "Lord, teach us to pray," it was because they had just watched him "praying in a certain place." [31] When he would teach his disciples an unforgettable lesson in humility and service, he "took a towel, and girded himself . . . and began to wash the disciples' feet." [32] He did not merely preach to publicans and sinners, he befriended them. He did not just talk about a better world, he healed the sick, forgave the sinful, and preached good tidings to the poor.

All teachers teach themselves and their own attitudes with inevitable success. Jesus was no exception. Indeed, he, more than any other teacher in history, cannot be separated from what he taught. What Albert Einstein taught about the nature of the physical universe is true or false regardless of who taught it. But what Jesus taught can never be considered apart from him. He did not just teach about love, he demonstrated it, saying, "Love one another, as I have loved you." [33] He did not just talk about God, he revealed him, saying, "He that hath seen me hath seen the Father." [34] Jesus was not only the greatest teacher who ever lived; he himself was the greatest lesson he ever taught.

Where others guessed, he seemed to know. Where they quoted authorities, he spoke with an authority born of an intimate knowledge and experience both of God and man.

A Saviour who would win the response of a scarred and bleeding world must himself have borne scars for the sake of men. Jesus' hands were pierced by nails as cruel men hung him on a cross. Men can say of him, "Surely he hath borne our griefs, and carried our sorrows." [35] A Saviour who would win the hearts of the poor must know the problems of the poor. Jesus' self-denial was so complete that he had no place of his own to lay his head. He knew the plight of the hungry; he felt the pangs of hunger to the point of wanting to perform a miracle to satisfy his hunger. He can promise us victory over sin; he himself met temptation and came *off* victoriously. Indeed, he is the only one in all history of whom it can truthfully be said that he was "in all points tempted like as we are, yet without sin." [36]

Jesus has a right to ask us to take up our cross and follow him; he accepted his own cross and died upon it. We can trust his promise of eternal life, for he himself tasted death, and yet rose victoriously from the grave.

To speak with authority, one must know his subject. Jesus, as no other person who ever lived, revealed the true nature of God. He knew the incomparable joy of intimate fellowship with God. He knew what it was to find God's purpose for his life through prayer. He knew the security that comes from a complete surrender to the will of God. He carried in his heart the confidence that he was the Son of God; God's chosen Messiah. He even knew what it was like in an hour of supreme trial to feel forsaken of God. But the crisis of the moment could not blot out the faith of a lifetime. His supreme faith in God came ebbing back as he gasped with his dying breath, "Father, into thy hands I commend my spirit." [37] Truly it has been said of him that in his life and death we have the "spectacle of a love that would not let go of man, and a faith that would not let go of God." [38] That love explains his every act. That faith stands forever vindicated by his resurrection from the dead.

Other great religious leaders may qualify at some of these points; only Jesus qualifies at them all. Others point to God. He brought God to men. Only he, therefore, deserves our unqualified allegiance forever. Isaiah dreamed of a day when the people who walk in darkness would see a great light. In Jesus that light has shined. What judgment men invite upon themselves and on their world if, because their deeds are evil, they continue to love "darkness rather than light." [29]

HIS PURPOSE IN TEACHING

~~~~~~

In Luke's account of the transfiguration, as translated in both the King James and Revised Standard Versions of the Bible, an arresting word is used in connection with Jesus' death. Speaking of that shining moment on the mountainside when Jesus was transfigured as he prayed, and when, for three of the disciples, the curtain of time itself seemed to be drawn aside, revealing to them a vision of heavenly visitors in conversation with the Master, the burden of that conversation with Jesus, Luke tells us, was "his decease which he should accomplish at Jerusalem." [1]

Accomplish! What a strange word to use in connection with anyone's death! and yet in Jesus' case how appropriate! For this word, so happily used by the translators, and appearing in such an unusual context, is suggestive of the fact that, far from being a tragic defeat, Jesus' death was to be a glorious accomplishment. His death, however, was but the culmination of a life given with utter self-abandon toward the achievement of his goal. What was that goal Jesus hoped to accomplish by his life, and supremely by his death?

No person ever lived with a more compelling sense of mission than did Jesus. "My meat," he declared, "is to do the will of him that sent me, and to finish his work." [2] Toward the end of his ministry, when he was tempted to deviate from his goal and to say, "Father, save me from this hour," [3] it was his sense of mission that held him steady. "But," he argued with himself, "for this cause came I unto this hour." Thus he met, and conquered, his temptation with the prayer, "Father, glorify thy name." Even his death he interpreted as being a part of the fulfilment of his mission. What, then, was that mission he felt he had come to accomplish?

During his ministry Jesus healed many bodies, but he certainly did not consider that the primary purpose for which he had come. On the contrary, he repeatedly expressed concern lest his healing ministry should eclipse in the minds of his hearers the more basic spiritual healing he had come to affect. Again, he has been called history's greatest teacher, but he did not come simply to add to the bulk of the world's knowledge. He knew that in the hands of unprincipled men even such a glorious possession as knowledge can become a dangerous thing. The Pharisees were learned men, but were part of the problem of their time. An associate justice of the United States Supreme Court recently observed, "It is the supreme irony of our time that the world needs to fear only the educated man." [4] Too often, knowledge, which should serve as a lever to lift men to new levels of life and understanding, has been used by some of its unscrupulous possessors as a cudgel to force men more illiterate than themselves into slavish subjection.

Not that Jesus would oppose the quest for knowledge. He would rejoice in it. "Come and see," [5] he invited those who sought more information about him. He never discouraged honest questions. After all, it was he who said, "Ye shall know the truth, and the truth shall make you free." [6] It is important to note, however, that this is not the entire quotation. While it applies to all truth, Jesus was careful in this instance to indicate the particular truth he had in mind, for he prefaced the statement by saying, "If ye continue in my word, then are ye my disciples indeed, and," he added, "ye shall know the truth, and the truth shall make you free." In other words, it was the knowledge of life's true meaning and purpose as revealed in him to which he was referring, the understanding and acceptance of which he said would really make men free. It was a knowledge of the love that motivated his life, and that he indicated comes from the very heart of God, to which he would call our attention.

Jesus came, therefore, not to make us more learned, but more loving; not to impart new facts, but to inspire new faith. It was with the realm of our relationships that he was primarily concerned—first to God and then to man. After all, facts, for all their importance, have no meaning until they are related to life. To a generation schooled in the scientific method of seeking and applying ascertainable facts, religion asks the questions: But how do you interpret the facts? By what standard, or standards, do you judge their significance and value? What moral purpose, if any, motivates you in your use of them?

It is not enough to make men better technicians; we must make them better men. To the scientists of our day, by whose work and dedication to their task Jesus would surely be thrilled, he would just as surely say, "Make this the first formula with which you experiment: Seek ye first the kingdom of God and his righteousness, and all the remarkable achievements of science will be added unto you as a blessing, not a curse, to mankind." To a reverence for accuracy, he would add a respect for ideals. To a world that prides itself on the speed with which men can travel, he would ask the direction in which they are going. To an age that brags of its knowledge of science, he would ask about its knowledge of God, and what difference that knowledge makes in how men live with one another and with themselves.

Perhaps no word in the English language more accu-

rately describes the true nature of Jesus' mission and
purpose as revealed by his life and death than the word "redemptive." Jesus came, as was said of him, to "save his people from their sins." [7] The redemptive nature of his mission
is revealed at the very outset of his ministry when he who
knew no sin requested of John the baptism that was meant
to symbolize the remission of sins in order that, by that
act, he might identify himself with the people in their deepest need. If ever there were any doubts in his mind as to the
redemptive nature of his mission, they seem to have been
swept completely away at the time of his baptism, when, in
response to his act of dedication, there came to him the
sense of absolute certainty concerning the role God intended him to fulfil. Whether anyone else heard the voice
or not, surely he did. "This is my beloved Son, in whom I
am well pleased." [8]

We tend to underestimate the soul-stirring nature of Jesus' experience on this occasion, because we fail to grasp
the graphic nature of the picture by which the Gospel
writers sought to describe it. They told of the "Spirit of
God descending like a dove, and lighting upon him." [9] We
tend to think of a dove as a bird that flutters gently to the
earth, whereas, some Bible scholars tell us that undoubtedly
the bird referred to in this connection is much more like our
swallow that swoops to the earth when it alights. In other
words, the Spirit of God came to Jesus in an overwhelming
rush to assure him beyond a shadow of a doubt that he was
God's chosen Messiah.

If this were true, Jesus knew and shared enough of the
messianic insights of the prophets to know something of
the role he would be expected to fulfil. His would be the
role of the Suffering Servant—a role in which he would be
oppressed and afflicted. In the words of Isaiah, many
would see in him "no beauty that we should desire him," [10]
as he sought to carry out God's redemptive purpose in the

world. His must be the way of supreme self-sacrifice. It must be the way of obedience and love. It would mean, that if men smote him on one cheek, he must be willing to turn the other cheek. It would mean the way of a seed which, except it "fall into the ground and die, it abideth alone: but if it die, it bringeth forth much fruit." [11]

But this is not the way of the world. The world puts primary emphasis on the fulfilment of physical and material needs. The world delights in the spectacular. The world tries to conquer by force, not love. It covets power, prestige, and wealth, even if it has to worship Satan to get them. These were temptations even for Jesus, and so he was "led up of the Spirit" into the wilderness "to be tempted of the devil." [12]

Could Jesus, in the face of what it would cost him, and in the face of Israel's clamor for freedom, give himself wholly to the establishment of a purely spiritual kingdom? That the struggle was not easy is indicated by the length of time it took him to resolve it. The issue was not settled until his body cried out for a miracle to appease its raging pangs of hunger as he gave himself, without thought of food or comfort, to the solution of his problem. At last it was settled. If Jesus received complete assurance of his redemptive role at the time of his baptism, he responded to it with complete commitment in the wilderness of temptation. Others might try to be conquerors. He must be Redeemer.

Having made the great decision, we find him declaring it. To Nicodemus, we find him explaining God's redemptive purpose for the whole world and his own part in its fulfilment. Having made the great commitment, we find him fulfilling his role by eating with publicans and sinners and declaring in defense of his action that "they that be whole need not a physician, but they that are sick"; and, further, that he had "not come to call the righteous, but sinners to repentance." [13] Thus he sought, not only by word of mouth, but by the alchemy of his presence, to give new hope and joy to those to whom life had been cruel, restrictive, and condemnatory; to give them a new sense of their worth and dignity as children of God as he sought, without discrimination, to draw them into the orbit of his love.

For Jesus came, as he said, to give life in a new and abundant sense to all who are dead to life's truest values and deepest joys; to add the dimension of spiritual hope and grandeur to all who are living stooped and constricted lives. John quotes him as saying, "I am come that they might have life, and that they might have it more abundantly." [14] And again we hear his cry, "Ye will not come to me, that ye might have life." [15]

In a world where Jesus knew men's spirits were meant to soar in living fellowship with God and in a mutually-rewarding fellowship with one another, he found people content, for the most part, to live a selfish, earth-bound existence—seldom, if ever, rising above the dull, mediocre level of material and physical satisfactions. Instead of love and understanding, he found millions living at the mercy of ruthless oppressors; crushed to earth by conditions they seemed powerless to change or control. Instead of lives overflowing with love and joy, he found them cramped with selfishness and pride, hedged in by jealousies and hates, burdened by anxieties and fears, and weighed down by sin and guilt. In the face of all this, Jesus came to call men to a way of faith and love that is possible only when men cease to live for themselves and begin to live for God; only when they cease to trust in themselves and put their trust in God. One of Jesus' most telling parables was told in condemnation of those who "trusted in themselves," [16] and who, therefore, thwart God's purposes and love both for themselves and the world.

The Gospels are full of examples of those who, through

contact with Jesus, began to experience more abundant life. The story is told of an artist who moved into a new community where his wife employed a local girl to help her with her work. One evening, as they were all standing on the porch looking at a beautiful sunset, the artist began to call attention to the various blends of color in the sky. Perhaps, like Archibald Rutledge, he described "the huge clouds smoldering, the long lanes of emerald light between them, then isolated clouds like red roses climbing up some oriel window of the sky, the deep refulgence behind it all." [17] At any rate, the girl suddenly asked if she might run home to tell her mother to look at the sunset. "Of course, you may," said the artist, "but your mother has seen hundreds of sunsets like that." "Oh, no, sir," replied the girl, "we never saw a sunset until you came."

Men could truthfully say they had never seen what life lived in the fulness of God's love and will could be like until Jesus came. The woman taken in adultery is an example. Here was a woman who, in order to find love, even if it had to be of an illicit sort, had thrown off the restraints of society and the moral teachings of her own religion. In doing so, she may have thought she was freeing herself, when, in reality, she was not only inviting upon herself the condemnation of the community but was fastening upon herself the fetters of guilt that sin always imposes.

But when Jesus made the woman free, she was free indeed, not only from external condemnation, but from sin itself—the sin she must have hated even when she felt powerless to reject it. She found that forgiveness and understanding were for such as she. Set free from the conflict that must have waged in her soul, she who had deserved punishment but who had received encouragement to make a new start instead, must have felt like saying, "I never knew what life lived free from the tensions of sin could be like until Jesus came."

The same can be said for the woman of Samaria. She, too, had defied the moral standards of her community; so much so that she chose to come to the well for water in the heat of the day rather than at a time when she would have to face the hostile, accusing stares of her neighbors. But after Jesus had talked to her, she went running to these selfsame neighbors to say, "Come, see a man, which told me all things that ever I did: is not this the Christ?" [18] We can well believe that, for her life began in an entirely new sense as the result of her conversation with Jesus.

We know too, that Zaccheus became a changed person after he met Jesus. Here was a man who thought he knew what life was. To him it was getting money and power, regardless of the methods one had to pursue to get them. But Zaccheus could not walk down the street without being conscious of the stares of hatred and contempt of which he was the target wherever he went. Then he met Jesus. And the impact of Jesus' personality and message on his life was so great that he did the unheard-of thing of offering to make fourfold restitution for all the money he had taken unjustly from the people. Money was no longer the all-important thing in his life. Now, as he walked down the street, conscious of the burden that had been lifted from his soul, Zaccheus could say, "I never knew life could be so wonderful until Jesus came."

Matthew was so grateful for the Providence that had caused him to be chosen as one of the disciples that he not only gave a dinner to celebrate it, but put the story of his call in the midst of a long list of miracles [19]—as if to say that, in his thinking, the fact that Jesus had chosen him to be a disciple stood on a par with some of the more obvious miracles Jesus had performed. Like so many thousands since his time, Matthew discovered that life abundant begins when a soul meets Jesus and surrenders to his claims and his way of life.

But what is this abundant life of which Jesus spoke? How does one experience it? Like any vital experience, it cannot be imprisoned in a definition any more than one can contain the fragrance of a flower in a butterfly net. Jesus did, however, at several points in his teachings, indicate something of what abundant living really means.

For one thing, abundant life is that quality of life that comes through placing one's trust in God and finding a sense of intimate fellowship with God. One can no more achieve abundant living by himself than he can lift himself by his own bootstraps. Abundant life, in the sense in which Jesus used the term, comes from such a vital trust in God and such a thorough commitment to his will that all of life becomes transformed by that relationship. It is the reward for living so completely within the consciousness of the love and will of God that nothing life can do to a person can destroy that trust. It offers the only security one can ever know that this world cannot take away: the security of trusting in a God whose love can never falter, and whose word can never fail.

It was precisely this feeling of security within the love and will of God that made Jesus' own sense of poise so amazing. His own life was based so completely on faith in God that even when the world was about to do its worst, he could still say to the disciples, "Be of good cheer; I have overcome the world." [20] Speaking of the faith of Jesus, one author has said, "Nothing gives greater evidence of Jesus' faith in God than his utter lack of despair. One wonders that he did not, at times, give way to what his brothers and sisters know as despair. But of that there is no suggestion in his gospel. In fact, it is a curious characteristic of his people that, just when, judging by every human consideration, they ought to be on the verge of despair, they always put it from them." [21]

Abundant life, then, is the reward of putting one's life

and trust wholly into the hands of God whose love was made visible to men in the person and ministry of Jesus. Through such love and trust life finds a new incentive. It takes on a new motivation. A person who lives abundantly tries to do what is right, not because the law says he must, but because his chief aim has become the desire to please God. The sense of God's approval becomes his chief joy. A lover does not consider it a chore to serve his beloved. In fact, he would be unhappy if he could not do so. A person who has seen God in the face of Jesus, who has come to know and love the God revealed in Jesus, sees religion not as an additional burden, but as the source of power and strength that enables him better to carry all of life's burdens.

When one's chief desire is to know and express the love of God, the world of others is brought, in a new sense, within his purview. What and whom God loves, that one begins to love also. This, too, contributes to abundant life, for, as Jesus said, it is in helping others to find life that we find a greater measure of it for ourselves.

Thomas Jefferson put the right to pursue happiness alongside the rights to life and liberty. The pursuit of happiness is probably the major pursuit of our time. Everyone is trying to pursue it in one way or another. Night clubs and taverns are full of people pursuing happiness. But people who pursue it find it an elusive goal; for true happiness is not to be had by pursuing it for its own sake. Happiness is a by-product of losing oneself in something greater than oneself. It comes more through giving than through getting. While some seek selfishly and fail to find a fuller life through conviviality and pleasure, others, like a young missionary giving herself in compassion to serve her fellow men in a bombed-out area of Japan, are able to write, "Each new day for me is a glorious new adventure." It was a true insight that led the author of

Hebrews to write of Jesus, "who for the joy that was set before him endured the cross, despising the shame." [22]

Jesus was right. It is they who love God and man who enjoy the greatest rewards. It is they who hunger and thirst for righteousness who shall be fed. They who drink of the waters of pleasure shall thirst again. They who live by a genuine desire to love God and serve their fellow men have within themselves an abiding faith and concern that are like a well of water springing up unto abundant life.

Obviously, if life is to be abundant, it must give promise of something more than the mere transitoriness of earthly existence. The most glorious life is lived under a shadow if at death it comes, all too soon and far short of its goals, to complete and final oblivion. Said Dr. R. E. Gaines, for more than fifty years a beloved professor of mathematics at the University of Richmond, on the occasion of his ninetieth birthday, "When you reach my present age you will understand that human life at best is very brief and wholly inadequate. In our early years, we dream of the things we shall do if we are spared for a reasonably long life, and then when we come to the end of the journey, we are shocked to discover that not half of these things have been accomplished. We should be in a state of hopeless pessimism but for the fact that human life on this planet is not the end but the beginning; all eternity is ahead of us." [23]

Jesus never conceived of life merely in terms of life in the body. He spoke explicitly of those "which kill the body, but are not able to kill the soul." [24] The ultimate purpose for which he said he had come was that men "should not perish, but have everlasting life." [25] But everlasting life is not to be thought of merely in terms of the future tense. In Jesus' vocabulary, the words "abundant" and "everlasting" seem to have been synonymous. The abundant life of which he spoke offers both the prospect of a present reality and a future reward. Its primary factor is not its duration but its quality; a quality based upon its relationship to God. Even in this world we understand the difference between duration and quality. Someone has slyly suggested that to be immortal a sermon need not be eternal. Without the prospect of a joyous relationship with God, a life of endless duration would be anything but a pleasant outlook, whereas, the experience of that relationship is something that can begin here and now as men put their trust in God and in the things of the Spirit as Jesus revealed them.

The rewards of such hope and trust, Jesus indicated, are peace and joy; a peace the world can neither give nor take away.[26] This is no mere shallow offer of "peace of mind" for those who close their eyes to the problems and suffering of this world and think only of God and heaven. The joy Christ would give is not, as some would accuse, an opiate to deaden us to life's ills. It is rather a divine antibiotic that offers healing for what has hitherto been incurable.

Certainly Jesus did not experience joy by avoiding life but by invading it with his gospel of truth and love. His peace and poise came from his absolute confidence that undergirding all he thought and did were the everlasting power and approval of God. Our confidence in the priceless rewards that Jesus promises us rises from our assurance that the God who revealed himself in Christ is not dead. He is not disinterested in what happens to us. Sin and death have no terrors for him. Time and eternity are his to command. To have such an assurance is to have peace in the midst of storm and joy in the midst of trial.

The tragedy is that so few reflect this joy. Maude Royden once wrote, "The very worst sin of most religious people is that they go about the world looking as if God were dead." And someone else has said, "Joy is the flag flying from the castle of the heart to show the king is in residence." What a pity if people who call themselves Christians fly the flag of joy at half-mast as if the King of heaven and earth were dead!

But if our hope and joy depend upon our relationship to God, it must be a restored relationship, since sin, by its vandal hand, has destroyed our relationship to God, and since all men are victims of what one author has called "the demonry of their own desires" that has set up a "dominion of sin within their souls." [27] Before men can experience the abundant life of which Jesus spoke, they must be free to experience God's fellowship; free to claim God's promises; free to love both God and their fellow men. Jesus came, therefore, to set men free from all that cripples and enslaves their lives. Most of all, he came to set them free from the deadly sin of pride and self-love with its evil spawn of prejudice and hate that clogs the heart and warps the judgment, and from which man by himself cannot rescue himself.

How much Jesus felt this to be his mission, and how much men are mastered by their pride and vindictiveness are indicated by an incident that happened in the synagogue in Nazareth. Jesus was home for a visit. As was his custom, he attended worship on the sabbath. An air of subdued excitement must have pervaded the congregation as he entered, for already his fame had spread the length and breadth of the land. One can imagine the light on Mary's face as she entered with Jesus and the fondness with which her gaze followed him as he took his place among the men.

Because of his fame, he was invited to read the lesson. Quickly he chose the place where it is written, "The Spirit of the Lord is upon me, because he hath anointed me to preach the gospel to the poor; he hath sent me to heal the brokenhearted, to preach deliverance to the captives, and recovering of sight to the blind, to set at liberty them that are bruised, to preach the acceptable year of the Lord." [23]

As he handed the scroll back to the attendant, we read

that every eye in the synagogue was fastened upon him as he started to comment. "This day," he declared, "is this scripture fulfilled in your ears." A gasp of surprised must have greeted this announcement. What was he saying? That he was sent to fulfil this prophecy? In a sense that is what the people wanted to hear. They were waiting for someone who could free them from all that which bound and enslaved their lives. Most of all, they wanted deliverance from the hated tyranny of Rome. How often they prayed for a leader who could rid them of the awful oppression of this cruel and hated enemy!

But that is not what Jesus had in mind. On another occasion he made it clear he had not come to umpire disputes between individuals.[29] Nor had he come to umpire disputes between nations. Jesus came to set men free from that which crushes them; for he knew that men are bound most of all by forces that spring from within the heart itself. He came to deliver men from the deep-seated causes that make men enemies of one another; to deliver them from the universal sin of self-righteousness and pride that makes them set themselves up as being better than their neighbors, and even to rebel against the authority of God himself. Jesus went on, therefore, to expose this unsurrendered prejudice and pride by reminding them that in the days of Elijah there were many widows in Israel who needed help, but it was to a widow in Sidon the prophet was sent. Also, there were many lepers in Israel in the days of Elisha, but it was to Naaman, the Syrian, that the prophet was directed.

How unerringly Jesus put his finger on the basic problem of their pride and prejudice is indicated by the violence of their reaction.[30] It was not just that he talked about a Sidonite and a Syrian, but that he implied that God's grace is equally accessible to those who are outside the Jewish law and tradition. To admit that would be to endanger the whole religious system on which their sense of national unity and pride were based. The tradition and the law meant everything to them. Of the spirit of forgiveness and reconciling love, there seemed to be little evidence among those who sought to kill Jesus; and yet Jesus knew they could never really be free until they were free of the fear and hate within themselves that set them against their fellow men and even prevented them from experiencing and reflecting the redeeming love of God.

For it was man's separation from God that concerned Jesus most of all. Man can never really be right with his neighbor until he is right with God. And he cannot get right with God until something is done about the sin in his life; something that only God can do. Since man cannot bridge the chasm between himself and God—he is neither good enough nor smart enough—God must bridge the chasm to man. The life and work of Jesus is that bridge. We can now approach God with confidence and trust, because he first approached us in Jesus. Jesus came, therefore, not just to save us from false ideas about God, but to save us from sin itself by lowering the bridge of God's redeeming love across the dismal moat of our stubborn sin and pride.

"The Son of man," Jesus said, "is come to seek and to save that which was lost." [31] And to be lost, Jesus made it clear, means, most of all, to be separated from the Father's love and his purpose for our lives; to be out of relationship with his redeeming, renewing power and presence. The sheep in the parable was lost, not just because it had wandered away from the fold, but because it had taken itself away from the shepherd's love and care. The coin was lost because it was no longer in the possession of the woman who owned it. The boy was lost because he had cut himself off from his father's love and care. He could not be found until he was willing to say, "I will arise and go to my father." [32]

It was precisely this outreach after the lost that distinguished Jesus' ministry as he sought in his life and death to reveal the divine initiative of God, who, as the great Physician, did not wait for people to send for the doctor, but who, in Christ, went out to seek and heal the sick. Jesus came, as he said, "not to be ministered unto, but to minister, and to give his life a ransom for many." [33] Both in his life and in his death he was like the shepherd going out to seek the lost sheep, the woman seeking her lost coin, the father seeking his lost son. For the shepherd did not wait for the sheep to find its way back of its own accord; he risked death to go out on the mountainside at night to search and find it. The woman did not wait for morning to come to see if the coin would turn up; she lit a lamp, and swept the room until she found it. The father did not wait until the prodigal son came in the front door before he rose to greet him; he watched for him, and "when he was yet a great way off, his father saw him, and had compassion, and ran, and fell on his neck, and kissed him." [34]

Dr. T. Z. Koo, well-known Chinese Christian leader, points out that in the East men do not run in public, or openly express affection in such a demonstrative way. It is not considered dignified. He believes, therefore, that Jesus' audience was amazed, even shocked, by this turn in the story. It was Jesus' way of illustrating the extent to which the father took the initiative to restore the son to full fellowship in the family. The father could not go into the far country and compel his son to come home—even God cannot coerce us into loving him—but when the boy returned with trepidation in his heart, his fears were swept away as his father, who had been watching and hoping for his return, ran down the road to greet him. Jesus came that we might know even in the far country that when we want to return to God's love, it is all right to come home; the Father is watching and waiting to receive us.

Obviously, Jesus could not have done this by his life alone. As Dean Pike reminds us concerning the cross of Jesus, "More has been accomplished for the good of man by his work in those closing hours than by the most free and active endeavor of anyone at any time in his life in all history." [35] Had Jesus lived only a perfect life, taught, and died a natural death, he would have remained only our highest example; which would have left the world worse off than it was before, for already there were men whose goodness very few could emulate. But because he followed God's will to the cross, Jesus became the world's Redeemer. For while his death was but the culmination of his life given with supreme self-abandon toward the fulfilment of his purpose, without his sacrificial death his life would have no power to redeem us from helplessness and sin. Without his life, the cross would have no meaning. Without his cross, his life would have no power to save.

The heart of the gospel is not the admonition to live like Jesus lived, although that remains our perfect goal. The heart of the gospel is the assurance that "God commendeth his love toward us, in that, while we were yet sinners, Christ died for us." [36] By his death, as he could not by his life, he defeated the powers of sin, and by his resurrection, he has given us our greatest basis for the hope that our "labour is not in vain in the Lord." [37]

But there is a further step. Jesus came not only to set men free from the dominion of sin by bringing them into a restored relationship to God that they might enjoy abundant life, but he came also to unite men into a living fellowship based on truth and love. In a world obsessed with the love of power, he came to create a fellowship that would reveal the power of love. In a world rife with suspicion and strife, he came to call his followers into a fellowship based on the truth of God as revealed in him. It was to this end that he promised his disciples the power and aid of the

Holy Spirit, who would unite them into such a living fellowship.

When Jesus stood on trial before Pilate, and Pilate asked him, "Art thou a king then?" Jesus answered, "To this end was I born, and for this cause came I into the world, that I should bear witness unto the truth. Every one that is of the truth heareth my voice." [38] This was a kind of power of which Pilate was totally ignorant. He thought chiefly in terms of controlling men by violence, or by the threat of its use. "Knowest thou not," he warned Jesus, "that I have power to crucify thee, and have power to release thee?" [39] But Jesus thought in terms of the power of truth and love to conquer where brute force is bound to fail. The power of armies! Pilate could understand that. That was tangible. The power of truth! That seemed intangible. What kind of a basis was that on which to build a kingdom? And so Pilate asked, in evident contempt, "What is truth?" [40]

Perhaps Pilate would have understood better what Jesus had in mind if he had been more familiar with Jesus' teachings. For one way to know what Jesus meant by the kingdom of truth is to know how he characterized the kingdom of evil. On one occasion he said the devil "was a murderer," and "There is no truth in him. . . . for he is a liar, and the father of it [lying]." [41] Thus he pictures Satan as being the direct source of violence and deceit.

Violence and deceit! How this old world has been undone by those twin demonic forces! These are the forces by which so many empires have sought to build their power. In our time we have seen two great political movements seek to rise to power by the use of these two diabolical methods: first naziism, and now Marxian communism. To Hitler a lie was not immoral if it served his purpose; in fact, he even considered it good if it could further his own ends. Ultimately, of course, these methods bring about their own destruction. In the meantime, however, they make those who have no compunction about using them all the more dangerous as a threat to peace and freedom. One thing is clear. We must not try to cast out Satan with Satan. To try to substitute cleverness for character or to exchange honesty for expediency would be to play into the very hands of the enemy and to endanger the spiritual foundations on which any decent and peaceful world must be built.

Jesus abhorred a lie. There was not a deceitful cell in his body. That is why we can trust him when he says, "I am the way, the truth, and the life." Indeed, Dr. Leslie Weatherhead points out in his book, *After Death*, [42] that the two basic reasons for believing in life after death are, first, the character of God—if God is like Jesus, he would never encourage us to hope for that which he knew we could not receive—and, second, the trustworthiness of Jesus. Jesus would not say what he knew was not true. And it was he who said, "In my Father's house are many mansions." [43]

Thus Jesus' teachings throw light on his ministry and his life gives meaning to his teachings. We may not understand all the reasons why Jesus had to die, or how his death contributes to our salvation, but we know some of the reasons for which he said he had come. He came, he said, to give life abundant and everlasting to those who are subject to sin and death. He came to set men free from the forces that destroy their lives and deprive them of their inner worth and of an eternal hope. He came, he said, to seek and to save the lost by bringing them into a restored relationship with the Father. He came, finally, to draw men into a living fellowship, or kingdom, based on truth instead of lies, and in which the spirit of vengeance and violence would give way to the spirit and practice of love.

The peace of the world, as well as of our own hearts, waits upon the realization of these goals.

IV.

THE MASTER TEACHER'S FAITH

~~~~~~~~~~~~~~~~~~~~~~~~~~~~~~~~~~~~~~

D r. W. A. Smart, noted Christian teacher and leader, tells about a woman who came to see him about her personal religion.[1] Harassed by religious doubts, confused by conflicting theological points of view, and yet impressed by the humanitarian aspects of Jesus' ministry, she said she had decided to forget theology and henceforth to make her religion simply an attempt to live like Jesus lived. When asked what she meant by that, she explained that just as Jesus went about doing good, so she would try to go about doing good. Jesus, in her thinking, seemed to have been reduced to little more than a glorified social worker. Her attitude seemed to reflect the words of the poet:

> I have no need of creeds,
> They but confuse the mind,
> For all the creed this old world needs
> Is that of being kind.[2]

Dr. Smart commended the woman for her ambition to live like Jesus lived. He pointed out, however, that in order to do so, God would have to become the most real factor in her life; so real she would never decide any issue without first referring it to his will; so real she would spend long hours in prayer seeking to know his will for her life. For, he went on to show her, one cannot understand Jesus, or why he did what he did, without understanding something of his sense of intimate relationship with God. "His life," says Dr. Smart, "was based on an implicit, unquestioning faith that back of this phenomenal world, and back of all history was the guiding hand of a Father God, a great Spirit of moral love, with which all life becomes divine." [3] That basic faith lies back of, and explains, everything Jesus ever thought or did. As a teacher of religious truth, he based his authority not on man-made arguments, but on his own experience of the empowering presence of God in his life. "The words that I speak unto you," he declared, "I speak not of myself: but the Father that dwelleth in me, he doeth the works." [4] His knowledge of God's will and his desire to do that will were, above everything else, the controlling factors in Jesus' life. To know and to do God's will was the all-consuming passion of his life.

The primary fact of the centrality of God in the life and teachings of Jesus is emphasized by practically every writer who seeks to interpret his significance for our day. In their book, *What Did Jesus Think?* Drs. Brown-Serman and Prichard say that the one thing that stands out in Jesus most gloriously is "his will to find and follow the will of his Father. To the verdict of that will," they add, "he refers everything. His whole life is summed up in the purpose, 'To do thy will, O God.' The unique moral factor in Jesus is the completeness of his identification with the Father." [5] For Jesus everything revolved around the reality and nature of God. To him God was not a problem about which to speculate, but a Power by which to live; not a force to be treated with casual indifference, but a Father to be trusted with confidence and love; not a cosmic bystander to be taken or left at will, but a creative Being who is the beginning and the ending, the center and the circumference, the source and the goal of all life. What God is and what he expects were, for Jesus, the determining factors for all of life.

How thoroughly the character and will of God served as the touchstone for everything Jesus thought and did is indicated by his teachings. Why, according to Jesus, should we strive to be perfect? Because God is perfect.[6] Why should we be willing to forgive others? Because God is willing to forgive us so much.[7] Why should we strive to love even our enemies? Because God "maketh his sun to rise on the evil and on the good, and sendeth rain on the just and on the unjust." [8] Why should we seek to reflect God's love? Because we should try to act as children of God.[9]

Dr. E. Stanley Jones once told of a bishop who decided to practice greater courtesy toward other drivers on the road, not only because it was safer, but because it made him feel more like a bishop. So, Jesus asks us to act in love, even toward our enemies, not primarily because of what it will do for our enemies, but because of what it will do for us. It will make us feel and act more like children of God, whose every act, including his judgments, is dictated by love.

Of course, the Christian message does not stop there. If it did, it would lead to despair instead of hope. Who can be perfect as God is perfect? Who can forgive as God forgives? The more we strive to obey God's will, the more we become conscious of our inability to do so. Haunted by our past failures, and conscious of our ever-present weaknesses, we would face ourselves and our future with utter despair were it not for the promise of God's help. It is precisely because we know we cannot save ourselves that we look for a Saviour. "Man's greatest need," as one book expresses it, "is not merely to be shown the pattern of God's will, to be exhorted to copy it, and at last to be convinced that happiness can never really be possessed until that consummation is achieved. The crying need of human nature is to be restored to a right relationship with God. Man needs to be forgiven." [10]

Jesus came to provide the assurance of that forgiveness. But having received the assurance of divine forgiveness if we seek it, man also needs to know the direction in which he should grow, the laws governing his growth, and the source and goal of a truly satisfying life. The answers to these, and all other questions, said Jesus, lie revealed in the character and purposes of God. Man's first quest, therefore, must be to know God and his righteousness. Everything else depends on that.

We have said that Jesus came to give life in a new and abundant sense to all who are dead to life's spiritual meaning and power; to release men from the deadly power of sin to dominate and control their lives; and, in a world of violence and deceit, to set them in a creative kingdom, or fellowship, based on truth and love. But how did he hope to accomplish these ends? How did he hope to do what the great religious teachers and leaders before him had not been able to do, namely, to liberate men from their sins and unite them in a fellowship of love and service?

To anyone who reads the Gospels, the answer is clear. Jesus did not try to accomplish these ends by giving men a new set of rules and regulations. They had enough of these already. Nor did he try to do it by giving them a series of pep talks on brotherhood. In fact, Dr. Ernest Ligon contends [11] that Jesus never talked about brotherly love, but about fatherly love; the kind of love a true parent bears toward his child, which, for most people, is the purest and most unselfish love they ever experience, and which, said Jesus, is but an intimation of the nature and greatness of the love God bears toward us his children. It was this love Jesus sought to make real. He sought to liberate men from their sins and bring them into a new relationship with one another by first bringing them into a new and transforming awareness of God as their Heavenly Father and of their fellow men as the children of God.

Moreover, Jesus sought to bring men into a new relationship with God by bringing them into a relationship of love and trust with himself. "Ye believe in God," he said, "believe also in me." [12] It was not what Jesus said about God that got him into trouble with the religious leaders of his day, but what he said about himself. It was because he said, "I and my Father are one," [13] and, "He that hath seen me hath seen the Father" [14] that they took such sharp issue with him. As Dr. James Moffatt points out, the distinctive note in Jesus' teachings about God is not that God is our Father, but that God was *his* Father.[15] It was out of this consciousness of his unique relationship with the Father that Jesus could speak with such confident authority as to the nature of God.

Jesus did not argue the existence of God for the same reason, one would suppose, that he did not argue the existence of the sun; he did not think it was necessary. One does not argue the existence of the sun to people who are seeing by its rays and being warmed by its heat. Similarly, Jesus must have felt one does not argue the existence of God to people who are surrounded everywhere with evidences of his judgments, his creative activity, and his love. Thomas Edison did not argue the possibility of electricity. He invented a light that revealed its power to produce incandescent illumination. Jesus did not set out to prove God, but to let the love and purity of God shine with perfect luminosity through his life.

For God, as Jesus pointed out, acts. He acts in nature. "Behold the fowls of the air: for they sow not, neither do they reap, nor gather into barns; yet your heavenly Father feedeth them." [16] He acts in history. The signs of the times, said Jesus, bear a revelation of the judgments and purposes of God more truly than the color of the sky fore-casts the weather.[17] Most significant of all, however, God acts with concern for human welfare. "If God so clothe the grass of the field . . . shall he not much more clothe you, O ye of little faith?" [18] He knows our needs before we express them. He sits in judgment over the nations, yet the smallest occurrence does not pass unnoticed by his ever-watchful eye. He notes the sparrow's fall, and num-bers the hairs of our head. He comforts those who mourn, gives rest to the weary, and stands revealed to the pure in heart.

Obviously, since God revealed himself through a per-son, he himself is Person; he has a personality to reveal. Thus the God we see in Jesus is intensely personal. He is not a mere abstract force operating impersonally in a me-chanical universe, but a self-conscious Being who feels, and thinks, and acts. He is not an entity to be revealed in a test tube, but a Reality to be experienced in the heart. Even if we could find some objective proof of God by means of the scientific method, we would not have found the real God as Jesus reveals him. For God is "Thou," not an "It." One does not discover the reality and worth of another person by mere scientific means, but through communica-tion, friendship, and love. And God is revealed to us through Jesus in a life of faith that brings us to the realiza-tion that when he speaks to us, it is always as a Person-to-person call.

Thus the God we see revealed in Jesus is not, as one confused student described him, an "oblongue blur." He is a living, loving Heavenly Father who hears and answers prayer. Indeed, Jesus could not have prayed as he did if he had not thought of God as being personal, since prayer would have no meaning except as it takes place between two beings capable of mutual understanding and response.

To depersonalize God would lead to a depersonalized

concept of life. This is exactly what has happened in a world that has come to depend so largely on the operation of machines. "Don't waste the time of the machine" was a sign posted in a factory during the war. Evidently, the output of the machine came first; human welfare seemed a secondary consideration. Millions of people today believe that economic determinism, or fate, or some other equally impersonal force determines the welfare and destiny of man.

Even in the realm of theology, there are those who have rejected the figure of anthropomorphism (God conceived in the form of a man), only to embrace what Dr. B. H. Streeter has called "mechanomorphism" (the universe conceived as nothing more than a vast, impersonal machine running according to powerful, but impersonal, laws in a colossal, but mechanical, process). Some even think of God as nothing more than the sum total of human hopes and aspirations projected against a cosmic background. It is difficult to see, however, how such a Sum Total (even if spelled with capital letters) could account for even our own weak personalities with their sometimes surprising capacity for faith and love, let alone the glorious personality of Jesus.

Ignatius Loyola once started to draw up an inventory of what he owed God that he might increase his sense of gratitude, but he never got beyond the first item—that of his own personality. That in itself was miracle enough to evoke a lifelong sense of gratitude to God. Impersonal forces, however powerful, could never account for the attainment of self-consciousness, intelligence, faith, and love as experienced by even the least of us, to say nothing of the incomparable personality of Jesus that shines out as the perfect example of what God meant life to be like.

To think of God as personal is not, as some would accuse, to be guilty of trying to make God in our own image.

It is to think of him in terms of the highest we know. The highest we know is not machines, however intricate they may be, but the people who invent them, operate them, and determine their uses; not laws, however just, but those who enact and enforce them; not flesh, but the radiant spirits of those who, often in spite of physical handicaps, live lives of courage and faith. No machine, however cleverly designed, can compare with its inventor. No body, however perfectly formed, can compare with the personality that expresses itself through the flesh. Nature's highest achievement is not a beautiful face, but a beautiful life. A physical presence his enemies could contemptuously describe as "weak," [19] pales into insignificance beside the faith and spiritual grandeur of Paul the apostle.

Personality is life's highest attainment. It is self-conscious and purposive. It is the highest fact within the realm of our experience, and, therefore, is the best clue we have as to the nature of ultimate reality. To say God is personal is not to limit him to our stature. It is to say that God is at least a self-conscious Being, capable of thinking, of willing, of loving, and who, as one writer puts it, is "the universal source of life, thought, righteous purpose and noble love." [20] As Dr. William Adams Brown so aptly sums it up, "God may be more than person; he may be other than person; he cannot be less than person. No word that is less than personality can so fittingly suggest what our experience of his working shows him to be." [21] The Christian would add that nothing less than the personality and work of Jesus can accurately reveal the true nature and love of God. Certainly, it was always in terms of a personal Being that Jesus thought and spoke of God, concerning whom his favorite reference was our "heavenly Father."

This is not just an academic matter. The whole meaning of life depends upon it. Without faith in a personal God, the whole concept of prayer would become untenable.

One could no more pray to a cosmic principle and expect an understanding response than he could expect a changing expression on the face of a "bloomin' idol made o' mud." As the gifted scholar, Emil Brunner, points out in his much-quoted book, *The Scandal of Christianity*,[22] if God were only a timeless idea, then the ultimate aim of life would be unity of thought; but if God is Person interested in all persons, then the aim of life is community. If the first concept were true, then life's most important factor would be knowledge. If the second is true, then life's most important factor is love. In the first case, God would be only the object of our contemplation, whereas Christianity presents him as the divine Partner who shares our life and endeavors.

For the God we see in Jesus is not only personal, he is knowable. He is not a God who hides himself, but a God who reveals himself to men. He hears and answers prayer. He responds to those who seek, reveals to those who ask, and opens to those who knock. He wants not so much to be explained as to be experienced. For while, in a world where materialistic communism seeks to promote atheism on a world front; where secularists follow a philosophy of practical atheism, living as if God does not exist or matter; and where people are sometimes confused by some of the teachings of science, it is important to know why we believe God exists, it is more important to *know* God. We must know him, not as a logical conclusion, but as a moral Force; not just in a syllogism, but in a satisfying faith that purifies the conscience, strengthens the will, and gives meaning and purpose to this life and hope for the life to come.

One can—indeed, one must—enter into a personal relationship with God. This was the lesson Jesus impressed upon the surprised Nicodemus. Nicodemus recognized Jesus as a religious teacher, albeit, a great one, but he was

unprepared for the lesson Jesus was to teach him. For
Nicodemus was the proud possessor of a great religious
heritage. He could claim Abraham as his racial and spiritual ancestor. Moreover, he had attained a high station in
life. He was a ruler of the Jews. But of a personal sense of
God's love and guidance, he seems to have had no knowledge. "How can these things be?" he asked when Jesus
sought to illustrate the activity of God's Spirit in the
human heart.[23] Jesus knew that for all his great learning
and experience, Nicodemus needed an understanding of
God that could change his life—that experience so vital, so
transforming, which Jesus spoke of as a new birth. And
this new birth could only be experienced by Nicodemus
as he would respond personally to God's will for his life
and become conscious, through Jesus' life and ministry, of
God's redemptive love and plan, not only for Israel, but
for the entire world.

For it was the world Jesus carried on his heart. While
he felt his mission was primarily to the Jews who, by reason of their religious heritage, were peculiarly fitted to receive it, the God of Jesus was in no sense provincial. "The
field is the world. . . ." [24] "God so loved the world. . . ." [25]
"Go ye therefore, and teach all nations. . . ." [26] This was
the framework of Jesus' message. He swept away all provincial ideas of God when he said, "God is a Spirit: and they
that worship him must worship him in spirit and in truth." [27]
Wherever men seek him "in spirit and in truth," there he
may be found. He cannot be fenced in by the stupid barriers erected in men's minds. His presence is not to be
limited to Mount Zion, or to Mount Gerizim, or to any one
place or church to the exclusion of all others. It is the sincerity of the approach, not the scene of the quest, that determines God's response.

Jesus was not the first to call God Father. The Jews
referred to God as Father long before Jesus did, and no

people in all the world have held a more exalted conception of the role of the father in the home than they. One trouble, however, was that they sought to limit the extent of God's family. They thought of God primarily, if not exclusively, as the possession of Israel, just as the Samaritans acted as if they had an exclusive claim on God's favor. The Jews prayed in effect, "Our Father, who art in Israel," just as the Samaritans prayed in essence, "Our Father, who art on Mount Gerizim"—just as we sometimes pray as if what we really meant is, "Our Father, who art a Baptist— or a Republican—or an American—or at least a White Man." But God is too big to be caught in the narrow confines of our little prejudices and dogmas. Jesus challenged all provincial thinking about God when he prayed, "Our Father which art in heaven." God's love transcends all earthly barriers as truly as the heavens transcend the earth.

That is not to say that all approaches to God are equally valid. It is not enough to believe that God is universal. We must know what he is like. For it is the character of God that matters most of all, and it is precisely at this point that Jesus, as no other, gives us our greatest light. He taught, both by word and example, that God's chief attribute is love; a love made real and credible to men by Jesus' life and supremely by his death on the cross. Men can now believe in such love because they have seen it demonstrated in a life. Any true parent could understand it if Jesus had said, "God so loved his Son, he would give him anything in the world." But Jesus said something infinitely more significant than that. He said, "God so loved the world, that he gave his only begotten Son. . . ." [28] As one writer has put it, one cannot look at Jesus, and especially at that sublime moment when he prayed for his enemies from the cross, without realizing that the universe that could produce such a life, and such a moment, has "an inexhaustible well of forgiveness" at its heart. [29]

We must not think, however, that Jesus entertained any sentimental ideas about the nature of God's love. Jesus' own life was so completely motivated by love, he could say to his disciples, "This is my commandment, that ye love one another, as I have loved you." [30] But he could also, on occasion, express righteous indignation toward them; and on one occasion, they saw him drive the money-changers from the Temple. Jesus made it clear that to love people means to hate everything that seeks to hurt or destroy them; everything that tries to exploit them for selfish ends.

The Pharisees accused Jesus of many things, but they never accused him of being soft. There are no sterner words in the Bible than some that fell from the lips of Jesus. Jesus leaves no doubt that God's love is consistent with his righteousness. Of one thing we can be sure. The God we see revealed in Jesus is not morally neutral. He cannot treat sin as if it did not matter. Forgiveness is not merely a matter of letting bygones be bygones. The God of the New Testament will not be satisfied with gifts of mint, anise, and cummin even though they be tithed. He wants judgment, mercy, and faith. [31] The promise of weeping and gnashing of teeth for those who misuse God's gifts; the awful warning that it were better that a mill-stone should be hanged about one's neck and that he should be drowned in the depths of the sea than that he should offend one of God's little ones, these do not sound like a God whose judgments are to be taken lightly, or with whose laws it is safe to tamper.

There is no better evidence of God's complete moral integrity than the cross. If God were morally neutral, if he could treat sin as if it did not matter, then the cross would not have been necessary. But a righteous God cannot close his eyes to sin. He cannot treat sin lightly. The cross not only reveals God's love for sinners, it reveals the seriousness with which God looks at sin. It reveals something of

what it costs a righteous God to forgive sin. If God is both
a righteous God and a God of love, then the cross was
inescapable.

A Southern professor, known for his outspoken admira-
tion for Robert E. Lee, used to ask his class the question,
"Can God tell a lie?" When a student would reply, "No,
sir," the professor would agree, "That's right. God can't
tell a lie. It would be contrary to his nature." Then the professor would amuse the class by asking, "Could Robert E.
Lee tell a lie?" If anyone answered, "Yes, sir," the professor would respond, "You must be a Yankee. Robert E.
Lee couldn't tell a lie. It was contrary to his nature, too."

At least the noted professor was correct concerning
God. God cannot, or will not, do anything that is contrary
to his nature as revealed in the life and death of Jesus. He
cannot treat sin lightly, for that would be contrary to his
nature. Jesus knew a righteous God cannot leave sin un-
challenged; cannot leave men at the mercy of such an ugly
thing as sin, so, even at the expense of the cross, he reached
out to draw men from its deadly grasp. Thus he revealed
God's earnestness in dealing with the problem of sin. In
the cross, God inflicts upon himself the penalty of rescuing
men from sin.

Jesus himself suggests an illustration at this point. In one
of his parables,[32] he likens sin to a debt, and says our debt
to God is like that of a man who owed another ten thousand talents (about twelve million dollars), which is another
way of saying that our debt to God is unpayable. Suppose
we owed a person that much money. And suppose that
when the time came to pay it, we were unable to do so because we were bankrupt. What would we do? What *could*
we do? All we could do would be to throw ourselves upon
the mercy of him to whom we owed the debt, hoping he
would be as lenient with us as possible.

But suppose, further, that the one to whom we owed

the money was so scrupulously honest that he felt every debt should be paid in full. What could he do? He might understand our plight. He might want to forgive us our debt. But twelve million dollars is a lot of money. Moreover, to forgive a debt is to pay it yourself. And yet, suppose that after a night of wrestling with his problem— a night in which he faced all the consequences to himself of forgiving the debt—he were to come to us in the person of his son to say, "I have decided to forgive you that debt, and will make the arrangements to cancel it." We could never know all it cost him to make and carry out that decision. All we would know is that our only right to hold up our head in society as a free person would be due to his act of unspeakable mercy.

This, of course, is only an analogy. We can never fully know all it cost a righteous God to forgive our sins, or how Calvary pays the debt for us. We can only accept Jesus' assurance of complete forgiveness for those who seek it through faith in the cross, knowing that our only right to hold up our head in eternity is the result of God's act of self-revelation and self-giving in Jesus.

For that is the kind of love Jesus came to tell us about, and, much more, to show us. God's love is self-giving love. It is what we might call missionary love—love that goes out in quest of the sinner. Montefiore, the great Jewish scholar, has said that this, to him, is the distinctive note in the teachings of Jesus.[33] Other religions teach the love of God. Only Jesus depicted it as going out after the sinner; taking the initiative for our salvation; offering itself as a ransom for the sins of the world. Such love is difficult to understand. It is even more difficult to reflect. And yet we must try, with God's help, to let our lives become channels through which such love can flow to the world.

For Jesus taught, in no uncertain terms, that to receive God's forgiving love, we must be willing to share it. It is

V.

HIS PERCEPTION OF MAN

~~~~~~

When rumors that William Carey was planning to publish a translation of the Bible in the Bengali language reached the ears of the Marquis Wellesley, brother of the Duke of Wellington, and Governor-General of India, he was greatly perturbed by the news. Protesting to his Rector, the Rev. David Brown, chaplain of the East India Company, the Governor-General stoutly insisted, "It will not do to allow it." When asked for his reasons, he replied, "But you know, sir, that the Bible tells us that all men are on a level; now it will never do to circulate that in this country. If the natives get the idea they are equal to us, farewell to British government in India." [1]

The Governor-General had read his Bible with greater discernment than many. Whether his conclusion was warranted—and history does seem to have borne him out—he was certainly right in saying the Bible teaches that God is no respecter of persons. [2] Moreover, one has only to read the Gospels to realize the importance Jesus attached to the individual. As someone has put it, to Jesus everybody was somebody. Some of his greatest lessons, such as, "Ye must be born again," and "God is a Spirit: and they that worship him, must worship him in spirit and in truth," were first entrusted to an audience of one, indicating something of the importance Jesus attached to the worth and need of a single soul. In a world where, to borrow a phrase from the blind man whom Jesus healed, so many people tend to see those who do not belong to their particular group or class as "men as trees walking," Jesus helps us, as he did the blind man, to see "every man clearly" as an individual in his own right.[3]

Jesus' approach to world problems was primarily in terms of individuals and their needs. He knew that society is made up of persons, each one unique in his own right. He recognized, however, that persons cannot be considered entirely apart from the social milieu in which they live and by which their lives are shaped. His condemnation of some of the social attitudes and practices of his day, such as the suppression of children, and the easy tolerance of divorce, shows his awareness and concern at this point. Where the Jewish leaders thought primarily in terms of the nation, he thought primarily in terms of persons. He knew that, to have a godly community, godly people must make it up; and while he had much to say about what a godly community would entail, he did not, in spite of his deep concern about such problems as the treatment of the poor, seek to transform people by changing social conditions. Rather, he sought to change social conditions by transforming persons.

In his inspired series of sermons on the character of Jesus, Dr. Charles E. Jefferson writes of Jesus: "When we discover his method, we discover that his supreme concern is for the rightness of heart of the individual man. This moulder of empires gives himself to the task of moulding individual men. This arch revolutionist starts his conflagration in the individual soul. He draws one man to him, infuses into him a new spirit, sends him after one brother man, who in time goes after a third man, and this third man after a fourth, and thus does he mould a chain by means of which Caesar shall be dragged from his throne." [4]

"Would you change the environment," he continues,

"then begin by the transformation of men; and would you transform men, then begin by a transformation of some particular man. It is by the changing of the character of a man that we change the character of other men, and by the changing of many men, we change the character of institutions, and ultimately of empires and civilizations. When Jesus says, 'Behold, I make all things new,' he lays his hand on the heart of a man." [5]

Jesus knew the needs and longings of persons because he himself was a person; a person who lived in humble circumstances, and who knew what it was like to live in a country oppressed by the weight of political and religious tyranny. As has been pointed out, it is the very basis of the gospel that when God chose to reveal himself supremely to the world, he did so in the life of a person. Not, as so many expected, a glorified, unreal person, but a humble, human person who began his life as a helpless infant, who as a child was subject to his parents; who "increased in wisdom and stature, and in favour with God and man;" who was tempted as we are tempted, thirsted as we thirst, wept as we weep, and who, when he was hung upon a cross, suffered and died.

The fact that Jesus was a person glorifies every person. The fact that he was a carpenter glorifies all honest toil. His having been a teacher glorifies the entire teaching profession, and every other ministry that seeks to serve as he served. Having given so much of his attention to individuals and their needs, he sets the pattern for us to follow in a world that tends to lose the individual by blending him into the blur of the masses.

This is a matter of supreme significance today. William Addison makes the charge that the great evil of our day is the destruction of personality. The world, he says, "offers much to man in the plural; it kills him in the singular." [6] We offer youth new opportunities in our cities where most of them soon become a part of the cities' "faceless millions." The growth of industry and urbanization has tended to rob men of their identity as individuals, and to lump them together in general categories: "management," "labor," "foreigner," and the like. Many fail to see the Negro as an individual, and see him only as a member of his race. Even preachers are sometimes tempted to think of people as material for their congregation instead of thinking of their congregation as a gathering made up of individuals, each with his own personal victories and defeats, problems and needs.

This question of the worth of the individual is highlighted in our day by the alarming spread of communism that frankly assigns the individual to a role subservient to the state. For centuries men have been asking the question, which comes first in importance, the individual or the state? The destiny of millions, so far as their earthly life is concerned, depends upon the answer that is given to that question, and yet the world is not yet united as to its answer.

Marxian communism frankly gives the place of first importance to the state, or at least to the Communist regime and those who control it. It would claim that the individual has only those rights and privileges the state permits him to have. But what the state gives, the state can take away. In a recent book on Russia, Lenin is quoted as saying that "the working class is quite unable to know its own interests, and consequently it must submit to the leadership and guidance of a self-chosen, revolutionary elite." [7] In consequence of this doctrine, the authors go on to show that he "regarded any manipulation of persons or groups as justifiable." [8] In other words, communism believes that the state, and particularly the party leaders who control it, and who assume, therefore, that they have a right to determine what is best for the masses, comes first. Whatever they do to maintain their authority and power is considered (by them) to be just and right.

Democracy, on the other hand, being based more nearly on the teachings of the Bible, takes violent exception to this doctrine. It believes that governments exist to further and protect the rights of their individual citizens. It believes there are some rights the state cannot take away, because the state did not grant them in the first place. They inhere in the individual by virtue of his relationship to God; by virtue of the fact that he is a child of God. Democracy, therefore, believes that governments should derive their power to govern from the consent of the governed; that if government is to be for the people, it must be by and of the people. In a world where communist influence is so strong, and where, even in our own country, it is so easy, especially in our large cities, for individuals to sink into anonymity, and to be considered en masse, we do well to consider the doctrine of the importance of the individual as viewed in the light of Christian teachings.

For the doctrine of the worth of the individual is directly related to faith in the reality of an infinite and loving God. If man's life is determined solely by economic forces, and terminated entirely by physical death, then his worth as an individual is greatly reduced. Even then, one wonders by what right one person or group of persons enslaves another. But if every person is equally a child of God, with a bit of eternity within him, then he cannot be treated as a mere pawn on a board to be shoved about at will by anyone who deems it his privilege to play chess with the lives of his fellow men. A recent article on the use of light in taking colored pictures declares, "There is no such thing as a green tree or a yellow lemon except when light is present." [9] And there is no such thing as the infinite worth of a human soul unless there is also an infinite God who loves men as individuals and grants them eternal life.

It is at this point we get our supreme assurance from Jesus. For there can be no doubt as to which way he would answer the question of the relative value between institutions and men. To him, every individual, regardless of nationality or moral condition, is first of all a child of God; a person who is the direct object of God's love and concern, and therefore takes precedence over every human institution. Every individual, regardless of who he is, is the creation of God and is made to carry out the purposes of God in his life and in the world.

A French historian is quoted as saying, "Men are insignificant; man alone is great." Jesus would never have agreed with such a conclusion as that. He never lost the individual in the crowd. He looked behind all man-made labels and saw each individual as a person in his own right in the sight of God. Indeed, the supreme sin to Jesus, short of contempt for the Holy Ghost, was contempt for personality. This is shown by his words, "Whosoever shall say [to his brother], Thou fool, shall be in danger of hell fire." [10] The word translated "fool" comes from an Aramaic root meaning "to spit." In other words, he who holds another's personality in contempt; who, figuratively, spits upon it, is subject to divine disapproval and judgment.

If Jesus' concept of the fatherhood of God can be considered the warp of his message, the derivative concept of the worth of the individual is certainly the woof of all he thought and did. For Jesus was constantly calling attention to the incomparable worth of the individual soul in the sight of God. God, he insisted, is so acutely aware of the existence and worth of each individual that the very hairs of his head are all numbered. [11] Though sparrows are considered of such little value that it takes two of them to be worth a mere farthing, yet not even a sparrow falls to the earth without the Heavenly Father's notice. [12] If God so notices a mere sparrow, how much more, said Jesus, he must notice a human soul. Indeed, Jesus insisted that a single soul is of such inestimable value that not all the material wealth of this world is to be considered fair exchange in return for it.[18]

Jesus never lost sight of the fact that everyone with whom he dealt was first of all a person. In the eyes of the community, Matthew's significance as a person was eclipsed by the fact that he was a publican. Jesus refused to let the community's evaluation of Matthew's occupation or reputation stand in the way of recognizing his worth as a person, or his possibilities as a disciple. In the eyes of her accusers, the fact that a certain woman had become an adulteress took precedence over the fact that she was a person. In Jesus' mind, though he did not condone her sin, he made sure to tell her not to repeat it; the fact that she was a person took precedence over the state of her morals, and so he gave her another chance. People then, as now, attached labels to other people, and then proceeded to deal with them in terms of those labels. Thus, regardless of a person's character or talents, he was thought of, first of all, as a publican, a Samaritan, a Jew, or the like, and was dealt with primarily on that basis. Jesus ignored such labels and insisted on dealing with persons as persons, each one unique in the sight of God.

Nowhere is Jesus' attitude toward persons better illustrated than in his attitude toward children. During the war, Sir Winston Churchill is said to have objected to the garbled language in a certain communication by writing across it, "Up with this I will not put." The disciples seem to have shared a similar attitude toward children, fearing lest they should get in the Master's way. Jesus rebuked such blindness in no uncertain terms, pointing out that children have an importance in their own right. In fact, he insisted that in some respects adults have more to learn from children than they from adults. "Whosoever shall not receive the kingdom of God as a little child shall in no wise enter therein." [14] By placing children in the midst of the disciples, Jesus placed children and their ways in the midst of everyone's consideration, and indicated that civilization itself is judged partly on the basis of its understanding and treatment of children.

What Jesus did for children, he did also for womanhood. Even today in non-Christian countries women are treated pretty much as the property of the father or husband as the case may be. In Moslem countries, a man can get a divorce by the simple expedient of proclaiming three times in the presence of a witness that he is divorced, whereas the wife has no such right, and, practically speaking, has little, or no, recourse to law.

A similar situation prevailed in Palestine in Jesus' day. In his teachings on divorce, Jesus not only struck a mortal blow at all easy-going attitudes toward marriage, but he also lifted the status of womanhood forever. In a day when a man could get a divorce for the most trifling reason (burning a meal was declared by one religious leader to be sufficient grounds for a divorce), the woman could not, under any circumstances, obtain her freedom from a villainous husband. Jesus condemned divorce, pointing out that marriage is God's idea. He instituted it. It is a sacred as well as an intimate relationship, and is never just an arrangement to serve the convenience of the man. Each is meant to be faithful to the other till death. Only as men and women enter marriage in that light will they try to make of it all that God intends it to be and treat each other with the consideration and respect each deserves.

Jesus' attitude toward people is further illustrated by his teachings concerning the sabbath. The attitude of the scribes and Pharisees toward the sabbath is indicated by an ancient statement that if the sabbath could be observed for two successive weeks in every detail as the law prescribed, salvation would come to Israel. But it wouldn't—not un-less people's hearts were changed and their motives were right. It was the meticulous attention to the details of the law that was stressed in Jesus' day. Violations were pun-ished. Acts of mercy and good will not specifically pre-scribed were frowned upon, and even forbidden.

In this case, as in all others, Jesus focused attention on its purpose; and its purpose, he made clear, was to exalt God by enhancing the spiritual growth and perceptions of men. "The sabbath," he declared, "was made for man, and not man for the sabbath." [15] He did not mean thereby to belittle the sabbath, but to magnify the importance of peo-ple. The observance of the sabbath was not to be thought of as an end in itself, but as a means for drawing people into a closer and more meaningful relationship to God. Whatever accomplished that end or was consistent with that purpose, was permissible, and even desirable, on the sabbath whether it was contained in the letter of the law or not. In sabbath observance, as in everything else, "the letter killeth, but the spirit giveth life." [16] The sabbath was never meant to be used as a club for controlling men and beating them into submission to priestly authority, but was given to men as a tool to be used to exalt the name of God and for the spiritual uplift of the human race.

The same can be said of any institution. Men were not put into the world merely that states might exist, that in-dustry might flourish, or even that churches might grow. It's the other way around. All these things have come into existence that man himself might develop and grow in his knowledge of God and in his ability to live with, and serve, his neighbor. When any institution, regardless of what it may be, ceases to minister to the needs of people or to con-tribute to the ennobling of life, it forfeits its right to exist.

Not that institutions are unimportant. Jesus was careful to point out that man must be related to his neighbor as well as to God. While it is important in a world where the doctrine is often denied or ignored to stress the importance of the individual, it must also be said that in order to be a person, an individual must be related to other persons. No one lives his life in a vacuum. It can truly be said that a person is known by the relationships he keeps. For each person lives his life in relation to a great many things. He lives in relation to his family, his work, his social groups, his community, his nation, his world.

As one lives life, he discovers the importance of living in relation to some great cause, and, if he is spiritually sensitive, he will relate himself to some church or religious group. Thus he will recognize that the supreme relationship in life, so far as his sense of values and his eternal destiny are concerned, and in the light of which all other relationships take on meaning, is his relationship, or lack of it, to Almighty God.

Life takes on significance and meaning in terms of that to which it is related. Letters of the alphabet, as used in an anagram game, each printed on a separate block, and thrown together in a box, make a meaningless jumble. But let them become related in the right way, and they become an alphabet, or they become words with meaning and significance. Relate words together, and they become sentences and paragraphs that convey thoughts and ideas. Let those thoughts and ideas be related to some great theme, and organized by a master in the use of language, and they can become a Shakespearean sonnet, a Lincoln's Gettysburg Address, a Churchillian phrase, a Pauline epistle, or a Sermon on the Mount.

Lives by themselves cannot develop in meaningful ways, but let them be related to one another in a family where there are love and understanding, and each life is enhanced and enriched by that loving relationship. Let them be related in a community, and schools, churches, hospitals, and other institutions and agencies become possible. Let them be re-lated in a nation, and national security and governmental co-ordination and oversight become possible. Men must now learn how best to relate themselves on a world basis so as to bring out the best in one another and produce a world of understanding and peace.

Of course, the manner of the relationship is extremely important. Christ's formula, not originated but stressed by him, is, "Thou shalt *love* the Lord thy God with all thy heart, and . . . thy neighbour as thyself." [17] Men can be related in an enforced collectivism that denies them indi-vidual freedom and initiative, or they can be related in terms of voluntary co-operation that makes for progress and yet allows the maximum measure of individual free-dom and growth. Certainly the relationship that encour-ages the greatest amount of creativity on the part of the individual is one based on co-operation and trust in the common quest for workable, but elevating, goals.

After all, there are only two ways of holding society together. One is the coercive way of a dictatorship in which the individual is told what he must think and do, and the other is the cohesive way of voluntary commitment to certain commonly accepted ideals and goals. The method of the first is propaganda and police action. The method of the second is education. In the latter method there is a mutual sharing of ideas, plus united, democratic action, both of which involve a mutual acceptance and sharing of responsibilities. Through education also we find that this type of social living and progress is made possible only by recognizing the importance of ideals and personal integ-rity. "Whatsoever things are true . . . honest . . . just . . . pure . . . lovely . . . and of good report" [18]—these are not just nice things to think about if one happens to be in the mood for them; they constitute the only basis on which a free and decent society can be built.

But these qualities are related to a higher norm. To be related only to the things of this world is to live in too small a dimension. Jesus recognized the importance of our human relationships when he called the disciples into a fellowship that was to be the beginning of his church, and when he repeatedly told them to love one another. But he also stressed the need to be related to a higher source of values and power than this world can provide. He used the figure of the vine. "As the branch cannot bear fruit of itself, except it abide in the vine; no more can ye, except ye abide in me. . . . for without me ye can do nothing." [19] Only as life partakes of the divine life and is pruned and purged of its human impotence and sin can it produce fruit that is to abide.

For this also needs to be said. Although Jesus, as no other, stressed the importance of the individual in the sight of God, he would never have been guilty of the modern error of taking too optimistic a view of human nature. "He knew what was in man" [20] is the way one Gospel writer summed up Jesus' ability to read character and to discern the deepest intents of the heart. Jesus never painted a false picture of human nature. He knew the degradation and shame of which human nature is capable. He knew man's deep self-centeredness and stubborn pride. After all, he had to deal with a Judas and a Caiaphas. He could forsee the weakness of Simon Peter and the culpability of a Judas long before any denial or betrayal took place. "If ye then, being evil—" [21] that was his appraisal of human nature. He saw the evil in men's hearts. And he knew how ugly sin really is. The odor of tobacco smoke is always more noticeable, and often more offensive, to a nonsmoker than to an habitual user of tobacco. Being sinless himself, Jesus would be all the more offended by the ugliness of the sin he saw in others. Indeed, he saw the sins that others were inclined to overlook.

It was not only that Jesus ate with people who were

known to be sinners that won for him the hatred of the "respectable" people of his day, but also because he told people who thought they were righteous that they were sinners. In fact, he said the sins of pride and hate can be a greater deterrent to the kingdom of God than the more overt sins at which society frowns. A thief knows he is a sinner. A self-righteous person may not recognize how sinful his own attitudes of complacency and pride may be. Thus he may block God's will for his life and for mankind more effectively than if his need for God were more visibly apparent.

Nevertheless, Jesus also believed there was something in every person worth dying for, something worth saving, or he would never have gone to the cross for the sake of the world. Jesus could read Simon like a book—so much so, he could predict with absolute confidence that when the pressure came, Simon would deny him. Yet Jesus still called him "Peter," meaning "a rock," thereby calling attention to the qualities of steadfastness he knew were mixed up with Simon's impulsive, and sometimes vacillating, nature. Jesus saw clearly the crack in Judas' armor, yet even at the end, in the very hour of Judas' perfidy, he called him "friend"—a word that must have stung Judas' conscience like a lash, but a term that also indicated Jesus' love for him to the end.

The story is told of an aged scholar who, many years ago, was exiled to another country because of his Christian faith. With no money or friends, the aged saint was found one day ill and alone in a strange city. He was taken to an institution where, thinking he was just a shiftless vagrant, one attendant asked in Latin, "What shall we do with this worthless fellow?" To which, to the surprise of those listening, the aged scholar replied, also in Latin, "Would you call one worthless for whom Christ was willing to die?"

In the light of Jesus' estimate of human worth as evidenced not only by his teachings, but by his willingness to die for men, each person should cherish his worth in the sight of God. One does not treat a Stradivarius violin as if it were a cheap fiddle. He prizes it, takes excellent care of it, guards it well, knowing it cannot be replaced, and, if possible, seeks to place it in the hands of a great artist who can bring out its tonal qualities. One should not treat his life, for the salvation of which Jesus was willing to pay such an awful price, as if it had little value, but should treat it as the precious possession it is, placing it in the hands of the Saviour who can bring out its highest possibilities. With his gifted imagination, Dr. Howard Thurman suggests that by his great love for us, through which he revealed his estimate of our worth, "Jesus has placed over each person a crown he will be all his life trying to grow tall enough to wear." [22]

A former student of Lafayette College, Larimore Foster, once sent his father a birthday telegram in which he said, "My most used criterion of self-criticism is: would that make me a little bit more worthy to be called—Tom Foster's son." [23] In dealing with our problems that call for personal decisions, we might well ask, Would that decision or act make me a little bit more worthy to be called a child of God? Or, to use Dr. Thurman's figure, Would it help me to grow a little taller toward the crown Jesus has placed over my head?

Furthermore, Jesus' estimate of human worth gives us a gauge for dealing with other people. If every person is a potential child of God, then everything that tends to deny or lessen human dignity and worth deserves our implacable hatred and opposition. Moreover, it tends to guard us against false pride in dealing with others. This is true even for the church, or perhaps we should say, especially for the church. The church must serve if its message is to be heard and heeded, but its service must never smack of con-

descension. Always it must be motivated by a genuine respect, as well as love, for people.

Again it is Howard Thurman who warns us that even
such a worthy enterprise as Christian missions can present
a subtle danger if it leads us, out of our greater knowledge
and abundance, to think of ourselves as being superior to
those to whom we seek to minister.[24] Rather, we must recognize our understanding and attainments as a part of
God's goodness and seek to share them with others who,
though less privileged than ourselves, are no less deserving,
and who, out of their own experiences and culture, also
have an important contribution to make to us.

People want to be loved for themselves. They do not
want to be objects of pity, but partners in love. "Are you
my friend because you want to save me?" asked a person
of an evangelist, "or do you want to save me because you
are my friend?" There is an important difference. As Dr.
Martin Buber points out in his brilliant interpretation of
our relationship to God and man,[25] people do not want to
be treated as an "it," but as a "thou"; not as a thing, but
as a person. The church must love people because they are
people, because they are the objects of God's love and concern, and because their needs and sufferings strike a respon-
sive chord in the heart of every true Christian.

Some years ago, a severe storm broke suddenly along
the coast of New England. The families of the fishermen
hastened to the wharfs to await anxiously the arrival of the
fishing boats. In one village all the boats were safely in but
one. No one seemed to know who had taken it out that
day, but obviously the boat was in trouble. Five fishermen
prepared to go back out on the tossing ocean to rescue the
fisherman in distress. Because of the danger, the mother of
one of the five tried to restrain her son from going. "But
Mother," he replied, "you always taught me to put the
other fellow first." And so, along with the other four men,

he went out to rescue—his own brother—whom neither he nor his mother had known was out on the sea that day.

The Christian faith tries to teach us that the other fellow, regardless of his racial or national background, is our brother in the sense that both are children of the same God. Here, for example, is a person who has stood critically aloof from the problems of organized labor. But his brother joins a labor union. He no longer thinks of labor as an impersonal entity. Now, when he thinks of labor, he thinks of his own brother. Now, when labor gets a wage raise, his own brother gets a wage raise. Now, when the union goes out on strike, he thinks of how his own brother will be affected by this action. So when a Christian thinks of labor, he is thinking of his brothers. When he thinks of management, he is thinking of his brothers. In the Christian sense, every war is a civil war in which brother fights against brother, since both are sons of the same Heavenly Father.

In his play, *The Skin of Our Teeth*,[26] Thornton Wilder imagines civilization prior to the glacial age. The Antrobus family (an Anglicized form of the Greek word *anthropos*, meaning "man") lives, according to the housing standards of that day, in a cave. The Antrobus children play with crude stone wheels and a baby dinosaur. But the glacial age is upon them. It is getting colder and colder. Fearing that the older people will soon be unable to withstand the weather and will die off, and yet hoping his children will survive the rigors of the age, Mr. Antrobus tries to decide what, in his opinion, is the most important discovery mankind has made that he might teach it to his children and thus try to perpetuate it for the race. He decides that two discoveries are pre-eminently important: the discovery, after centuries of trial and error, that two times two equals four, and the invention of the wheel. And so, in every way he can, he seeks to impress the importance of these two achievements upon the minds of his children; and as the curtain goes down on the first act, he is talking about the value of the multiplication tables and the importance of the wheel.

Science and invention are important. No one in his right mind would disparage the contributions they have made to mankind. Without them, we, too, would have to go back and live like cave men again. But in the face of modern weapons of destruction (and Wilder leads to this in his play), it will take more than science and invention to save us. It will take faith in, and an understanding of, one another, plus a willingness to live together as children of God, each willing to recognize the worth and importance of the other.

One day Jesus was asked what he considered the greatest commandment that had come to man. He replied by stating they are two, so completely interrelated they can never be separated from each other. One is to love God with all our heart, and the other is to love our neighbor as ourselves.

The future life of man, so far as his life on this planet is concerned, depends on how soon and how well he learns to understand and abide by these two commandments. And how soon he does, depends largely upon how soon he grasps the truth of God's redemptive love as revealed in Jesus. Therefore, Christians have a special responsibility to try to bring this about by being witnesses to the love and message of Jesus in a world that faces the dire prospect of atomic destruction. But atoms can only destroy if hateful men make them do so. As someone has said, it is now Christ or chaos. Only as men learn to see life through his eyes will they really see the God who can save them, and realize their own deep need and worth of being saved.

THE THEME OF HIS TEACHING

Each day, in thousands of Christian churches or homes across the land, there are those who, in public or private worship, bow their heads and repeat the Lord's Prayer. In doing so, they give voice to the familiar plea, "Thy kingdom come. Thy will be done in earth, as it is in heaven." [1] For many—perhaps for most—it means little more than the parroting of an oft-repeated phrase. Perhaps here and there is someone who pauses to ask, What do these words mean? What is the kingdom of God, and how does it come? Am I ready for its coming? What changes would God want to make in me to prepare me for its coming? Miss Margaret Slattery contends that if Christians really stopped to think about what it implies, both in personal living and in human relationships, most of them would not be nearly so eager to pray for the coming of God's kingdom. "Thy kingdom come—but not now" [2] is the way she thinks most people would pray if they were really honest with themselves and faced the implications of what God's reign in the lives of men would mean.

One cannot study the teachings of Jesus without being impressed by the sheer number of times he mentions the kingdom of God. Even the most cursory reading of the Gospels reveals what a prominent role the concept of God's kingdom played in his thinking. At the outset of his ministry, Mark tells us, "Jesus came into Galilee, preach-

ing the gospel of the kingdom of God." [3] In his first sermon of which we have any record, Jesus took as his text,
"The time is fulfilled, and the kingdom of God is at hand:
repent ye, and believe the gospel." [4] He taught his disciples
to pray that God's kingdom might come on earth as it is
in heaven. An amazing number of his parables have to do
with the kingdom of God. He said, "Seek ye first the kingdom of God, and his righteousness." [5] His teachings
abound with references to the kingdom of God. He believed that he had come to inaugurate that kingdom. One
can no more deal with the teachings of Jesus without facing the problem of what he meant by the kingdom of God
than he could jump into water without getting wet.

But what did Jesus mean by the kingdom of God? What
is its nature, and how is it to be achieved? These are questions about which the greatest Christian scholars are by no
means agreed. Nevertheless, some things Jesus had to say
about the kingdom of God stand out so clearly in his teachings that even he whose eye runs through the pages of the
Gospels can read with some degree of discernment concerning the nature of God's kingdom and how it is to be
realized. What, then, are some of the implications for us
today in Jesus' teachings concerning the kingdom of God.

As any student of the Old Testament knows, the teachings of Jesus concerning the kingdom of God were presented against the background of the Jewish expectation
of a messianic reign. This was both a help and a hindrance.
It was a help because it afforded a framework in which
Jesus could present his concept of the kingdom. He could
build upon the expectation that had already been aroused
in the hearts of the people by the teachings of the prophets. This expectation had become so vivid that any mention
of the kingdom of God would immediately capture the
people's attention. It was a hindrance because, in their
minds, the thought of the kingdom of God was inseparably

bound up with their desire to regain their national independence. The concept of the messianic kingdom was, for the Jewish people, so heavily weighted with political connotations and the desire to get vengeance on their enemies that, in spite of Jesus' efforts to explain the spiritual nature of his kingdom, they still thought of it in terms of a temporal state. How thoroughly even the disciples missed the point of his teachings is shown by the fact that their very last words to Jesus were the question, "Lord, wilt thou at this time restore again the kingdom to Israel?" [6] Like those who cannot see the forest for the trees, they could not see the spiritual nature of his kingdom because of their preconceived political notions concerning it. Their hearts turned back with such wistful longing to the days of Israel's emergence as a nation under David, they could desire nothing better for themselves and their land than the recovery under a new David of Israel's independence as a political state.

But the kingdom of God as Jesus conceived it is not political. It cannot be identified with any temporal order patterned after the kingdoms of this world. It cannot even be equated with our American way of life. "My kingdom," said Jesus to Pilate, "is not of this world: if my kingdom were of this world, then would my servants fight." [7] And while such a kingdom seemed unintelligible both to Jew and Roman alike, its power has outlived the marching legions of the Caesars, and will outlast all the would-be imitators of Rome. Its symbol is not a sword, but a cross. Its warfare is not waged on battlefields, but in the hearts of men. It wins its victories not by killing men, but by giving them life. Its borders run not between nations, but between truth and error, light and darkness, love and hate.

The first thing to remember about the kingdom of God is the obvious, but ofttimes forgotten, fact that it is God's kingdom, and cannot, therefore, be brought in merely by the efforts of men. Men are neither good enough nor smart enough to usher in such a kingdom by themselves. It can only be brought to pass by God's power and love working in and through the hearts and lives of men. In the last analysis, the kingdom of God is not an achievement but a gift. "Fear not, little flock," said Jesus, "it is your Father's good pleasure to give you the kingdom." [8]

When the Rev. H. R. L. (Dick) Sheppard was the rector of St. Martin's-in-the-Field in London, it is said his doctor advised him to take two weeks off to rest. Thinking he could not possibly comply with such an order since the work of his parish called for his personal supervision, the beloved rector fell asleep and dreamed he died and went to heaven where he was ushered into God's presence. But God seemed very much upset about something; so much so that one of the angels asked him if anything were wrong. To which the Lord of the dream replied, "Yes, I don't know what I'm going to do. Dick Sheppard is going to take two weeks off."

The point of the story is obvious. It is not so much God who is dependent upon us to bring in his kingdom as we are dependent upon him. Our responsibility is to trust him and to let him bring in his kingdom through us. Perhaps if men realized this more, they would strive less and pray more, not for God to do our work for us, but that when we are used, we might be used by his Spirit.

This does not mean, as some have contended, that we are to sit idly by and wait for God's kingdom to come. The New Testament does not contain such counsel as that. Jesus never said the future belongs to the passive. The same God who spoke to Moses to say, "Speak unto the children of Israel, that they go forward," [9] has spoken more strongly to us through the parable of the buried talent.[10] There is no place for buried talents in a world that is in such desperate need of help. After all, God works through human instruments to achieve his purposes and will. What other medium has he for making his presence and purposes felt than the hearts and minds of men? Our hands must serve him, but he must supply the purpose and the power. We must invest our lives in his service and let him declare the dividends. We must march on in faith and trust him to part the Red Sea of whatever difficulties may seem to us to be an impassable barrier to the achievement of his purposes among men.

This is the point many of the Jews seemed to miss. As Paul was later to put it, they looked for a sign; [11] and the sign for which many of them looked was a heaven-sent leader who, by his supernatural power, would superimpose his kingdom upon the world and restore Israel to power. Luke specifically says that the disciples expected the kingdom to come as a sudden manifestation of God's power.[12] But the kingdom of God, as Jesus explained, does not come that way. It is not something that can be imposed, even by divine power, upon a reluctant world. God's kingdom is of the heart, and must develop from within the hearts of men. "The kingdom of God," said Jesus, "cometh not with observation: neither shall they say, Lo here! or, lo there! for, behold, the kingdom of God is within you." [13] And whether he meant from within the heart, or, since he was speaking to the Pharisees, from within their midst, it still requires spiritual vision to perceive it.

The Greeks also missed the point; for they, as Paul also declared,[14] were enamored of wisdom. They wanted to argue their way into the kingdom of God. They were more interested in examining a syllogism than in experiencing salvation. They wanted to be convinced mentally rather than to be changed morally. Like the scribe who asked Jesus about the greatest commandment, they wanted a religion that would not demand too much of them. For when the scribe commented on Jesus' answer to his question, he was careful not to commit himself too far. He did not say "my" God or "my" neighbor. Even when he used the possessive, he kept it in the third person as if to keep his commitment at arms length. And Jesus, noticing he answered "discreetly," told him he was not far from the kingdom of God, but yet not in it. He knew the answers, but not until he was really willing to let love be central in his relationship to God and his fellow men could he truly enter into the kingdom of God.[15]

For one does not experience the kingdom of God merely by knowing *about* religion as a scholar might know about the literary excellence of the Bible, but by living in terms of a genuine faith as a devout Christian turns daily to his Bible for guidance and strength. For faith, as Dr. Kirsopp Lake reminds us, "is not belief in spite of evidence, but life in scorn of consequence," or as Dr. Elton Trueblood simplifies the definition, "Faith is not belief without proof, but trust without reservations." [16] Faith is revealed in commitment to a cause, not in controversy over the relative merits of the commandments. It conceives of religion in terms of ardent discipleship, not just an academic discussion. Anyone can argue about religion, but the kingdom of God calls for those who will act in faith on the understanding of God that is made possible through the life and work of Jesus.

One difficulty in presenting the concept of a spiritual kingdom to the Jews lay in the fact that they were trained to think more in terms of the nation than of the individual. As Dr. Hillyer Straton states it, "The old Israelistic covenant with Yahweh was a covenant with the race. The new covenant which Jesus came to establish is one with the individual." [17] To the average Jew, the coming of the kingdom meant the time when the Jewish people would come into their own in a political, as well as a religious, sense. In order to be saved, one must become like a Jew. But

Jesus showed that all men, the Jew included, must be born again in a spiritual sense, since all men stand under the judgment of heaven for their sins and must, therefore, re-establish fellowship with God by repentance and faith.

Some years ago, when the late Mrs. Annie Armstrong was president of the Women's Missionary Union of the Southern Baptist Convention, she visited Romania. Finding herself in a small village just before Easter, she tried to find out where the Baptists were planning to hold their Easter sunrise service out on the mountainside. The person of whom she inquired could speak English, but was unfamiliar with the term "Baptist." In trying to describe them, Mrs. Armstrong mentioned the place where the Baptists ordinarily worshiped. As she did so, the man's face lighted up, and said, "Oh, you mean the Repenters!"

Certainly no one group holds a monopoly on the need to repent or on the experience of regeneration, but it is to the everlasting credit of the little Romanian group that it had so emphasized the need for personal repentance and faith that its members were known in the community as the "Repenters." For repentance and faith are the first steps one must take in order to enter the kingdom of heaven.

But a kingdom is not made up of one person, but of many. Nor can it be established by law alone, but by mutual respect and love. A kingdom is made up of those who are bound together by a common loyalty to the king, and who, because of that relationship, try to love one another. For if faith in God is the air men must breathe in order to live in the kingdom of God, love, both for God and man, is its climate. This is one of the major emphases of the New Testament. The kingdom of the Old Testament was a kingdom of law. The kingdom of the New Testament is a kingdom of love. It is based upon God's love for men as expressed in the life and work of Jesus. It is expressed in the love Christians are expected to bear, not only toward God, but toward one another. Love for and within the fellowship is one of the evidences of a valid Christian experience. "We know," writes one of the New Testament writers, "that we have passed from death unto life, because we love the brethren." [18] The kingdom of God, therefore, is expressed in a fellowship of those who, through faith in Christ, have been drawn into a new allegiance to God as King, and to one another as brothers in the faith.

In his book, *God Was in Christ*,[19] Dr. D. M. Baillie suggests that God's intention for the human race can be illustrated by the picture of children joining hands in a circle to play a game, each facing the center where the leader stands to direct the play. In similar fashion, God meant for members of the human race to join hands in a great circle of love and service, each facing toward the center where God shines as the eternal Light. By facing him, each is able to see not only the Light shining in the center, but the way it falls on the faces of those in the circle. In other words, each person begins to see others as God sees them and so is better able to begin to play the game of life according to the rhythm of universal love.

But, says Dr. Baillie, something has gone wrong. Instead of facing the Light, men have turned their backs on God. Standing in that position, they neither see the Light at the center nor the faces in the circle. All they see is their own shadows; the shadows of their own insecurity, fear, and pride cast upon the world, and the shadows frighten them. So they break hands, and in an effort to forget the shadows, each dances a little faster, but the shadows only become the more frightening.

In that kind of a world, says Dr. Baillie, God is trying to create a smaller circle that will demonstrate to the world how God means men to live together. First, he tried to create such a circle with the children of Israel, but in spite of its great lawgivers and prophets, Israel failed him. Now he is trying through the message of the gospel to draw all men into a fellowship known as the church that can present to the world a living witness to the power of God to unite men's hearts across the barriers of their human differences.

In a sense, the Christian church can be defined as a fellowship of those who, through faith in Christ, have experienced the redeeming love of God. The church does not do the redeeming. That is the work of the Holy Spirit. But the church is the fellowship through which the redeeming love of God can do its work. The church is not an exclusive club for the benefit of its members, but a fellowship of the concerned as it seeks to enlist all men to discipleship to Christ, and to draw them into its healing and revitalizing embrace. Indeed, the New Testament speaks of this fellowship as the very medium by which the Holy Spirit is to be mediated to the world.

At one stage in their development, John explains the impotence of the disciples by saying, "The Holy Spirit was not yet given." [20] The power of the Holy Spirit could not yet be given as the means, for its expression was not yet established. The disciples at this point were still a group of quarreling, self-seeking individuals, each interested in his own selfish ambitions. It was not until Pentecost, when, through faith and prayer, they prayed themselves into a united fellowship that the Holy Spirit came with transforming power. Jesus once said, "Where two or three are gathered together in my name, there am I in the midst of them." [21] The number is secondary. It can be, but need not be, limited to two or three. It can be two or three hundred. Though not so easy, it could even be two or three thousand. For wherever men join their hearts in a fellowship of faith and love, there the spirit of Christ can be revealed to the waiting world.

Obviously, there is a requirement for entrance into this fellowship. It is faith in Christ; faith that in him, God has spoken with definitive clarity and power. Here was no mere itinerant preacher moving about Palestine, able to turn a neat phrase, and exercising far in advance of his time a knowledge of the principles of psychosomatic medicine. Here was God's answer to the sin of the world and to the needs of men. Through this life, as through no other, God had chosen to speak—to enter in unique fashion into the affairs of men to rescue them from their blindness and sin.

This was the point at which Jesus started to build his church—the point of Peter's confession, "Thou art the Christ, the Son of the living God." [22] Not that Peter's experience was complete at this point. He had been converted to the person of Christ. He still needed to be converted to the program of Christ. It was long after his confession of Christ that Jesus could say to him, "When thou art converted, strengthen thy brethren." [23] As the Scriptures themselves make clear, Peter's larger conversion came through the fellowship when Paul "withstood him to the face, because he was to be blamed," [24] and when he needed a special vision to open his eyes to further truth concerning the Christian approach.[25] But Peter had made the right start. Believing in the person of Christ as God's answer to the need of the world, he could go on to help build the fellowship.

To believe in Christ is to surrender to Christ. And one way to surrender to Christ is to become a part of the fellowship of the church of Christ that through that fellowship, Christ can reveal more of himself to the believer, and through the fellowship of believers, to the world.

Not that the church as we know it is identical with the kingdom of God; it is much too imperfect for that. Nevertheless, it is the one institution that is trying, with God's help, to incorporate into its life and fellowship something of what Jesus must have meant when he talked about the kingdom of God. Perhaps if Jesus were here today, he would use the word "fellowship," or what is becoming an increasingly used word, "community," instead of the word "kingdom." In our world the word "kingdom" has lost much of its former prestige, whereas the words "fellowship" and "community" convey to the modern mind more of what Jesus must have meant when he preached the gospel of the kingdom. Indeed, Jesus indicated in his great prayer for the disciples that the miracle of Christian fellowship that unites men in a common bond of faith and love across the barriers of their many differences is to be one of the most convincing evidences to a doubting world that the Christian message is not just man-made, but is divine in its source.[26]

There will be many who will say that the Christian fellowship with its present-day multiple divisions is a poor witness to the unifying power of the Christian faith. With much of this charge, Christians can only agree with deep humility and shame. There is, however, a deep, underlying unity of faith and purpose that is often hidden from those who see only the surface confusion of many denominations and sects. A garden is not made up of one kind of plant, but of many. Pull them up, however, and one finds that beneath the surface of the soil their roots are intertwined. So it is with the Christian fellowship. In spite of many surface differences, there is a deep, underlying unity that is revealed in a growing sense of co-operation and mutual commitment.

Something like that has been happening between the various branches of the Christian church. In their beginnings, many of the leading branches of the Christian church were quite far apart, often because of national or sociological reasons, quite as much as theological reasons, if not more so. But as they have gone along in history, many of the major denominations have tended to get closer and closer together until now, theologically speaking, there are few real differences between them as they seek to bear a common witness for Christ, at the same time showing that the answer to the world's ills is not to be found in an enforced uniformity that robs individuals or groups of initiative and freedom, but in a unity of spirit and purpose that permits each person to worship God according to the dictates of his own conscience, and yet binds the hearts of all true Christian believers together in Christian love.

Obviously, an experience of the kingdom of God requires one to live in terms of its demands on his life. Needless to say, this is where the going gets tough. The word "Christian" is both a noun and an adjective. One experiences its meaning as a noun when he yields himself by faith to the claims of Christ upon his life. But to experience its meaning as an adjective, to grow increasingly Christian in one's thought and life, is a lifelong process. It can only be done with God's help, just as it requires deeper insight than that of which mere "flesh and blood" are capable [27] to discern Jesus' true significance in the first place. One of the requirements, for example, of a person who is trying to live as a member of God's kingdom is that he try to love his enemies. But, as Dr. Charles A. Ellwood reminds us, "To love our enemies becomes possible only when our whole being becomes sublimated and reorientated by a strong religious emotion." [28] To build a Christian home, young people need love to help them face up to its problems as well as its joys. To build the kingdom of God, one must love God, for only through such love will he experience the transformation of life and attitudes that makes him want to have a part in helping to build God's kingdom.

To live in terms of the kingdom involves risks. Jesus said it would. "Behold," he told the disciples, "I send you forth as lambs among wolves." [29] Someone referring facetiously to Daniel's experience said one cannot open his window to the east without sticking his neck out. In more dignified fashion, Dr. Kirby Page has summed up his impressions of Jesus' message and method by saying: "After years of contact with human suffering, and long vigils of brooding over human agony, Jesus came out of obscurity with a flaming new message and program: the purpose of life is to help create the family of God, where all men will dwell in filial relation with the Father, and with brotherly affection for each other; the method by which the desired end is to be reached is to live constantly as a good member of God's home, live day by day as if the ideal society had already been achieved; run the risks, accept the penalties, and rely upon this manner of life for the victory." [30]

But whatever the risks involved, Jesus said the possession of the kingdom of God is worth all it costs. It is like a "treasure hid in a field; the which when a man hath found, he hideth, and for joy thereof goeth and selleth all that he hath, and buyeth that field." [31] Or it is like a "merchant man, seeking goodly pearls: who, when he hath found one pearl of great price, went and sold all that he had, and bought it." [32] The reward overshadows the sacrifice as one gives up lesser satisfactions for the supreme satisfaction of knowing he is within the love and will of God.

The kingdom of God is what Jesus said it was, the exchange of lesser values for the highest value; the exchange of lesser joys for the supreme joy of knowing Jesus and sharing the Christian's hope. He who would claim the rewards of the Christian gospel must accept the disciplines of the Christian life. He must give up that which is incompatible with the Christian spirit and purpose. If he would claim Jesus as Saviour and Lord, he has no other choice but to follow his teachings and obey his commands.

The question may be asked, Does that not place limitations on one's freedom? Of course it does! A married man is no longer free to date any woman who might happen to catch his eye. He has pledged his love and fidelity to one person for the rest of his life. Both his wife and society have a right to expect that he will live up to that promise. To break it is to invite the condemnation of God and the censure of society. But only as he is willing to forgo the privileges of bachelorhood is he free to enjoy the richer rewards of requited love and married life. Only then is he free to experience the joys of creating a family and home. He gives up the passing pleasure of an evening's date for the joy of a lifelong companionship with the one he loves best, and the bright prospects of children and of family life. The kingdom of God is like that. One surrenders the selfish freedom of self-will for the joyous freedom of living as a child of God. One gives up striving primarily for treasures that "moth and rust doth corrupt" for treasures that time or eternity cannot dim. One gives up the short-lived pleasures of holding on to sin for the undying joy of a hope that cannot fade.

One of the poets has stated it this way:

> If, in that secret place
>   Where thou has hidden it, there yet is lying
> Thy dearest bitterness, thy fondest sin,
>   Though thou hast cherished it with hurt and crying
> Lift now thy face,
> Unlock the bolted door and let God in
> And lay it in His holy hands to take. . . .
>
> (How such an evil gift can please Him so,
> I do not know)
> But, keeping it for wages, He shall make
> Thy foul room sweet for thee with blowing wind
> (He is so serviceable and kind)
> And set sweet water for thy thirst's distress
> Instead of what thou hadst, of bitterness:

Who would not pray away his dearest sin
To let such service in.[33]

A young girl was persuaded to teach a Sunday school class of junior-age boys. But since she had never made a full commitment of herself to the Christian way of life, she asked to be allowed to give up the class on the grounds that she did not know where she was taking the boys. When asked what she meant by that, she replied, "I guess I don't know where I'm going myself." She was persuaded by the counsel and prayers of her pastor not to give up the class, but to give herself in complete surrender to Christ. A new experience came into the young woman's heart and a new note into her teaching. As a result of that new note, nine of her boys were led to make a profession of faith in Christ as their Saviour. On the morning the nine boys were received into church membership, the minister spoke of the influence of the young teacher in the lives of the boys. After the service, a friend of the girl rushed up to her and said, "I'd give my life for an experience like you have had this morning." To which the young teacher quietly replied, "That's what it takes, but it's worth it."

It costs to follow Jesus, but it's worth it. It may mean giving up some of the treasures of this world, but it's worth it to know the peace of mind which is the supreme treasure. It may mean being scorned for our ideals, but it is worth it to know a joy unclouded with regrets. It may mean the abandonment of questionable pleasures, but it is worth it to exchange the burden of a tortured conscience for the joy of self-respect. It may endanger our popularity to fight the entrenched forces of prejudice and evil in the world, but it is worth it to know we follow the example of him who cleansed the Temple. It may mean bearing a cross, but it is worth it to anticipate the crown of life he has promised.

One further point needs to be mentioned concerning the

kingdom of God. Jesus plainly taught that we can experience the kingdom of God here and now. He just as clearly taught that the kingdom of God will only be realized in its fulness when God himself perfects it at the end of the age. When will that be? Jesus did not say. On the contrary, he specifically discouraged speculation on that point. "Of that day and that hour," he declared, "knoweth no man, no, not the angels which are in heaven, neither the Son, but the Father." [34]

Dr. H. E. Dana was one of the careful students of the life of Jesus in recent years. Conservative in theology, he brought to his study of the New Testament the patience and equipment of a true scholar. In a brief study book,[35] he issues this warning. Speaking specifically of Matthew 24–25, where Jesus speaks of the end of the age, Dr. Dana writes, "The interpretation of it has been difficult for the best minds of all Christendom, and therefore one should always approach it with humility and avoid treating it with dogmatic certainty." Jesus' teachings about things to come, he goes on to point out, were "not to satisfy curiosity about the future," but rather "to safeguard faith."

Jesus knew the trials his disciples would be called upon to face. He knew how they would be tested. But they must not falter. The future is in God's hands. He will win the ultimate victory. Those who are faithful to the end will share the victory with him. The main thing is to be ready. To delay casting one's lot with Christ is dangerous, for God's patience does not last forever. The door of the bridegroom closes, and the golden opportunity to serve him may never be recalled.

Dr. James H. Franklin, former president of Crozer Theological Seminary, was addressing an audience of youth. He had been picturing the kind of a world this would be if the kingdom of God were fully realized—a world of peace and good will; a world of love and understanding; a world of liberty and justice for all; a world in which men would love God with heart, soul, mind, and strength, and their neighbors as themselves. Lifting his head as if he were peering into the future, he remarked as he sat down, "The kingdom of God in the sense in which I have been speaking is out ahead. We will not enter it in our lifetime. But please God when we fall, let us fall with our faces toward it."

The kingdom of God *is* out ahead. It is here, and yet eternally coming. Only God himself knows how and when it will fully come to pass. We will not fully experience it in our lifetime. But, please God, when we fall, let us fall with faith in its coming, and with our faces turned toward it.

VII.
A NEW KIND OF DISCIPLESHIP

A teacher cannot function without pupils. How else could he teach? And Jesus was no exception to that rule. He, too, needed disciples, or learners, with whom he could share his message. Of course, the whole region in which he traveled was his classroom. Wherever he went, he found those who would listen to him. Fortunately for us, since he left no writings of his own, some of those who heard him had retentive memories, and later made a record of what they remembered. But out of the vast multitude of those who heard him, Jesus chose twelve to be his special pupils; twelve who could assist him in his ministry and with whom he could carry on an intensive program of teaching and training; twelve who could be his daily companions and whom he could train to carry on his task when he had to lay it down.

That Jesus chose the kind of persons he did to be his disciples is revealing. Judged by the standards of worldly success, they were an unlikely lot with whom to begin such an important enterprise as the Christian movement. In the world of their day they were nobodies; just ordinary lay-men, although perhaps not so ordinary as we sometimes think, or Jesus would not have chosen them. But certainly they had no special theological training for their task. Some were fishermen; one was a tax collector; two were such hot-headed youths they earned the nickname "Boanerges," "sons of thunder." These were some of the candidates Jesus chose with whom to entrust the message of the gospel and the birth of the Christian church. To the leaders of their day, they must have seemed like very unlikely "branches" to carry on the life of the "True vine." Who but Jesus would have guessed that some of them would put forth such vigorous tendrils of faith and fortitude that not even Rome, with all its ruthless pruning, could cut away the vine of the Christian church from the arbor of that ancient world.

But why did Jesus choose the twelve he did to be his disciples? Why, if he wanted to impress people with his message, did he not try to include some "big names"; people of recognized power and authority who could have loaned added prestige to his efforts?

One answer, of course, is that people who are already established in positions of privilege and power do not readily respond to a revolutionary movement, and Jesus' program was revolutionary. It was not just a new patch on an old garment. It was a new garment patterned after a new concept of God and man rather than after the old dictates of the law. But Dr. Walter Rauschenbusch, in his book, *The Social Principles of Jesus*, suggests another reason why Jesus may have chosen the type of men he did to be his disciples.[1] He suggests that in a world of widespread political and religious oppression, one of the chief reasons Jesus may have chosen such humble men to be his disciples was that, among other things, he wanted to initiate in the world a new order of leadership—a leadership that would serve and not exploit—and so he chose as his disciples persons who were not already spoiled by the possession of power.

This is an interesting suggestion, for Jesus came into a world in which leadership was conceived largely in terms of issuing orders and expecting people to obey them; of holding people down and climbing up on top of them to a position of power and authority. "Ye know," he declared to the disciples, "that they which are accounted to rule over the Gentiles exercise lordship over them; and their great ones exercise authority upon them." "But," he added, "so shall it not be among you: but whosoever will be great among you, shall be your minister: and whosoever of you will be the chiefest, shall be servant of all. For even the Son of man came not to be ministered unto, but to minister, and to give his life a ransom for many." [2]

Here was an amazing formula for success. The way to succeed, said Jesus is to serve. The way to be first is to be last.[3] The way to find life is to lose it.[4] The apostle Paul summed up Jesus' approach to life by saying, "For ye know the grace of our Lord Jesus Christ, that, though he was rich, yet for your sakes he became poor, that ye through his poverty might be rich." [5] Jesus taught that real leadership comes from trying to understand people's problems, identifying one's self with their needs, sharing their load, and thereby trying to lift them up to a new life and a new hope. "Except a corn of wheat fall into the ground and die," said Jesus, "it abideth alone: but if it die, it bringeth forth much fruit." [6] Only as life is invested in a worthy cause can it produce worthy dividends. Only as a person denies himself in the service of God and his fellow men can he grow in spiritual power and become the means of bringing about greater good in the world.

Jesus not only called men to such leadership, he set the example. In a recent book, a church member complains, "The trouble with our church is there are no surprises in it." [7] Certainly that criticism could never have been made of the life and ministry of Jesus. His life was full of surprises. It began as a surprise. A Saviour born in a stable! It continued to produce one surprise after another. His crucifixion was a most surprising end to a life dedicated to truth and service. His resurrection was the supreme surprise of the ages. His entire ministry was a surprise in that he claimed to reveal the very heart of God, and yet did so as a humble teacher and healer of men. In all history there is no greater surprise than this, that when God chose to reveal himself fully to men, he did so in one who chose the role of a servant.[8] God girded with a towel! What greater surprise can you have than that? And yet we read that Jesus, "knowing that the Father had given all things into his hands, and that he was come from God, and went to God . . . took a towel, and girded himself . . . and began to wash the disciples' feet." [9]

A former student of the late Dr. Rufus Jones tells of a time when a famous English scholar came to deliver a series of lectures at Haverford College. While a guest on the campus, he was entertained in Dr. Jones' home. The first night after the guest had retired, Dr. Jones noticed, on going to his own room, that the guest had left his shoes in the hallway. Having traveled in Europe, Dr. Jones knew what that meant, and so the next morning the guest found his shoes freshly polished. That same thing happened every night during the week. As he was leaving, the noted English scholar took a coin from his pocket and asked Dr. Jones to give it to the person who had shined his shoes each night. With a wry smile, Dr. Jones pocketed the coin, and the guest returned to his own country without guessing that each night that week his shoes had been shined by a scholar more famous than himself. A gifted artist could do no better than to paint a picture of Dr. Rufus Jones polishing another's shoes with a picture in the background of Jesus washing the disciples' feet.

When the church loses its urge to serve, it loses its power to save. That is, it loses its power to speak with an arresting and effective voice. For though its minister speak with the combined eloquence of Phillips Brooks and Charles Haddon Spurgeon, though its organist play Bach with the touch and understanding of a Schweitzer, though its choir sing like a choir of angels, if a church loses its concern for ministering in the name of the humble Christ to the needs of sinful men, its services of worship become mere religious concerts, and not the means whereby people are made aware of the judgments and mercy of God. When a church becomes preoccupied with its own prestige and ecclesiastical patterns, when it becomes callous to what happens to people, when it loses vital touch with the sick and sinful, the suffering and the sorrowful, then it ceases to serve as the voice of God calling men to repentance and faith.

It was precisely at this point Jesus took such sharp issue with the organized religion of his day. The church had ceased to be what Dr. Elton Trueblood calls "the fellowship of the concerned." [10] Jeremiah had said, "Oh that my head were waters, and mine eyes a fountain of tears, that I might weep day and night for the slain of the daughter of my people!" [11] Joel had said, "Let the priests, the ministers of the Lord, weep between the porch and the altar, and let them say, Spare thy people, O Lord." [12] But the tears had ceased to flow. The religious leaders of Jesus' day had become so concerned with maintaining their own prerogatives, they failed to minister to the needs of the people. As Jesus put it in a stinging rebuke, "They bind heavy burdens and grievous to be borne, and lay them on men's shoulders; but they themselves will not move them with one of their fingers." [13]

The story of the Good Samaritan was not, as so many have tried to make it, a treatise on race relations. In a sense, the Samaritan was not of another race. The story was, for the most part, a stinging indictment of the religious leaders of that day for their lack of concern for a beaten and bleeding world. The priest and Levite were held up to scorn not because they were a priest and Levite, but because, as representatives of religion, they passed by on the other side of the road from a beaten and bleeding victim, which was exactly what organized religion was doing. It had become so preoccupied with its own prerogatives and with the meticulous observance of the law (its attitude toward sabbath observance is indicative) that it had lost a vital concern for men who were hungry,[14] and even resented the healing of a crippled man on the sabbath day.[15]

The story of the prodigal son was told quite as much to call attention to the attitude of the elder brother as it was to reveal the compassion of the father. This story was told, not to the disciples, but to the Pharisees. Not many of Jesus' parables have an allegorical significance, but surely there is an implied meaning to this one. The prodigal son is poor, foolish humanity that has left his father's home, and is starving for the life that satisfies. The father's heart is broken, but his compassion is unceasing, and his joy knows no bounds when the son returns. The elder brother represents the leaders of Judaism in Jesus' day; spiritually proud; their hearts no longer sensitive to the desperate plight of the world; thinking only of their own rights and of what they thought they had a right to expect from the Father's hand.

"When we cease to bleed," said Dr. John Henry Jowett, "we cease to bless." And when the church ceases to care for lost men; when it becomes more interested in extending itself institutionally than in lifting fallen humanity and helping them to discover and develop Christian experience and character in depth, it ceases to function as a channel of God's blessing and forfeits its claim to genuine moral leadership in the world.

The church can claim only one right, and that is the right to represent the ever-living Christ in his ministry of love and service, and to present the claims and promises of Christ to sinful men. The church must give of itself that men may live. The cross is not extraneous to life, but central. It is not just an isolated event in history. Its shadow falls across every Christian heart and congregation to show that we are expected to demonstrate its meaning and power by our willingness to take up our own cross and follow Jesus.

How else can we reflect the measureless compassion of Jesus? For while he was the world's greatest teacher, it was not a mere passion for truth but a love for men that drove him on. "When he saw the multitudes, he was moved with compassion on them because they fainted, and were scattered abroad, as sheep having no shepherd." [16] When he looked down on the rooftops of Jerusalem, the city that was the pride and joy of every Jewish heart, he wept. He saw not its grandeur, but its greed; not its shining turrets, but its sin; not its palaces, but its people living under the tyranny of both church and state, and out of his great heart was rung the cry, "O Jerusalem, Jerusalem, thou that killest the prophets, and stonest them which are sent unto thee, how often would I have gathered thy children together, even as a hen gathereth her chickens under her wings, and ye would not!" [17]

Dr. F. W. Boreham tells of going to Dundee, Scotland, to try to find out from those who knew him something of the secret of the power of Dr. Robert McCheyne's preaching. The old sexton of the church led him to the desk where Dr. McCheyne had prepared his sermons, and invited him to sit down. "Put your elbows on the table," said the sexton. "Now put your face in your hands and let the tears flow; that's the way Dr. McCheyne used to do." [18]

Contrast this with the blasé attitude of the modern world that reads news of the most devastating disasters without hardly batting an eyelash—unless, of course, it is someone who is known personally who is involved. We are a long way from thinking of all men as we think of those who are close to us, or of saying with Jesus, "Whosoever shall do the will of my Father which is in heaven, the same is my brother, and sister, and mother." [19]

But how to achieve the compassion of Jesus—that is our problem. Someone has said, "You cannot extemporize character." Neither can one feign compassion. Sincere compassion is not something that can be worked up at will. It must be genuine, or it is nothing.

Part of Jesus' tenderness came from actual contact with people and their problems and needs. He not only thought about the problems of publicans and sinners, he ate with them, and saw life through their eyes. Thus he saw them not as a problem, but as people who needed his love and consideration. He saw at firsthand the problems of the poor and the handicaps under which they lived, as well as the frustrations they constantly experienced. He knew from actual experience what it was to be hungry and to have no place to lay his head. He knew, too, the temptations of the rich, for he talked with them in their homes. He met the halt, the maimed, the blind. The blows that fell on their hearts fell on his own. He could not separate himself from the needs of men. He knew their sufferings too well to be callous to their plight.

Where Jesus did not actually see their suffering, he had the imagination to visualize it. He could see the sin and sorrow hidden by the rooftops gleaming in the sun. To him statistics on crime, poverty, and disease would not be mere figures on a page. He would have the imagination to see the suffering and tragedy they represent. In his play, *Saint Joan*, George Bernard Shaw has the English chaplain, after the burning of Joan of Arc, seek forgiveness for his part in sanctioning her death. When asked by Cauchon, the Bishop of Beauvais, why, if he felt it was so wrong, he had given his approval in the first place, the chaplain replies that he had not known how awful it is for a person to burn to death until he saw her body consigned to the flames; whereupon, the Bishop remarks sadly, "Must, then, a Christ perish in torment in every age to save those that have no imagination." [20]

Moreover, Jesus deepened his sense of compassion by prayer. He brought the needs of humanity before the throne of God in earnest prayer. He could say to Peter, "I have prayed for thee, that thy faith fail not." [21] One cannot pray for another without becoming more deeply concerned about the one for whom he prays. In the long vigils of prayer when Jesus brought the needs of the world to the attention of his Heavenly Father, his own heart must have been more deeply stirred, and he was made even more sensitive to the needs around him. In these moments of quiet communion, he saw human life as God sees it, and the love of God in him stirred to express itself in a ministry of healing and redemption. Thus he was led to identify himself with men in their needs and to die for their salvation.

Christ still calls us to a leadership of compassion and service, but we do not face the task alone. His promise is, "Lo, I am with you alway, even unto the end of the world." [22] We need not—we must not—depend upon our own strength and wisdom alone. Jesus did not merely say to his disciples, "Follow me, and be fishers of men." He said, "Follow me, *and I will make you* fishers of men." [23] The promise of his help makes the difference. He does not call us to a task to desert us. As someone put it, with better insight than grammar, "Whatever God calls you to, he will give you strength for."

It was this note of divine help John stressed so tellingly in his prologue when he wrote, "As many as received him, to them gave he power to become the sons of God, even to them that believe on his name." [24] Power to become! What an exciting promise! And yet that is our hope. To those who put their trust in Jesus, to them he gives power to be-

come what they could never be without his help. To Paul
he gave power to become a great apostle. To Francis of
Assisi he gave power to become a gentle saint. To Kagawa
he has given power to become a Christian leader whose life
and influence have overflowed the borders of his own land
to bless all who know of him and his work in the slums of
Japan.

Today Christ still gives power to those who believe in
him sincerely and seek to follow him. To some he gives
power to become effective and inspiring preachers and
teachers. To some he gives power to become outstanding
Christian laymen. To some he gives power to become
Christian parents and wives and husbands. To all his true
followers, he gives power to become an influence for righteousness out of all proportion to their recognized importance in the world.

Christ does not expect the impossible. He asks us to follow him one step at a time. When a woman who was threat-
ened with invalidism asked her doctor, "How long will I
have to lie here?" the experienced doctor wisely replied,
"Only a day at a time." Jesus calls us to follow him one
step at a time. He may ask us to take some steps the world
may not like. They may even lead to a cross. Ultimately,
they will lead to a crown. If we do not follow Jesus, to
whom else shall we go? He, and he alone, has the words of
eternal life.

REFERENCES

CHAPTER I

1. John 3:2
2. Luke 23:23
3. Jeremiah 37:17
4. John 5:39
5. John 16:13
6. John 16:2
7. John 14:6
8. For an interesting discussion of this, see *The Seven Christian Virtues* by Hugh Ross Williamson (New York: The Macmillan Co., 1949), p. 15
9. Luke 16:1–8
10. Luke 18:1–8
11. Arthur J. Gossip, *In the Secret Place of the Most High* (New York: Charles Scribner's Sons, 1947), p. 27
12. W. A. Smart, *The Contemporary Christ* (New York: Abingdon-Cokesbury, 1942), p. 139
13. Romans 5:8
14. Isaiah 59:1
15. John 12:32
16. 1 Corinthians 15:58
17. Said in an address before Northern Baptist Convention, 1948
18. Ecclesiastes 1:17–18
19. For a discussion of this, see John Knox, *The Man Christ Jesus* (Chicago: Willett, Clark & Company, 1942), pp. 43–44
20. Charles A. Ellwood, *The World's Need of Christ* (New York: Abingdon-Cokesbury, 1940), p. 43
21. John 3:2
22. Mark 12:37
23. Matthew 7:28–29
24. Luke 4:32
25. John 7:46
26. John 6:68
27. Luke 6:46
28. Matthew 7:24–27

CHAPTER II

1. W. A. Smart, *The Spiritual Gospel* (New York: Abingdon-Cokesbury, 1946), p. 125
2. John 14:11, e.g.
3. Luke 24:8

CHAPTER II (Cont'd)

4. John 1:12
5. Matthew 9:36
6. Matthew 9:36
7. W. M. Grant, *The Bible of Jesus* (New York: George H. Doran Co., 1927), p. xvii
8. Luke 24:27
9. Zechariah 9:9
10. Matthew 21:9
11. W. L. Stidger, *Sermon Nuggets in Stories* (New York: Abingdon-Cokesbury, 1946), p. 9
12. *Ibid.*, p. 9
13. Stanley Brown-Serman and H. A. Prichard, *What Did Jesus Think?* (New York: The Macmillan Co., 1935), p. 35
14. Charles Francis McKoy, *The Art of Jesus as a Teacher* (Philadelphia: Judson Press, 1930), p. 66
15. Quoted by Charles A. Ellwood in *The World's Need of Christ* (New York: Abingdon-Cokesbury, 1940), p. 65
16. For an illuminating treatment of some of the deeper meanings of the Lord's Supper, see *The Altar Fire* by Olive Wyon (Philadelphia: Westminster Press, 1954)
17. 1 Corinthians 11:24
18. John 7:17
19. Luke 10:3
20. Luke 10:4
21. Luke 10:17, 21
22. John 14:6
23. Job 10:20
24. Matthew 19:14
25. Isaiah 5:1–7
26. John 15:1
27. J. R. Dummelow, *One Volume Bible Commentary* (New York: The Macmillan Co., 1908), p. 666
28. Matthew 11:29
29. Matthew 16:13–15
30. John 16:12
31. Luke 11:1
32. John 13:4–5
33. John 15:12
34. John 14:9
35. Isaiah 53:4
36. Hebrews 4:15
37. Luke 23:46
38. Richard Roberts, *The Ascending Life* (New York: The Women's Press, 1924), p. 43
39. John 3:19

CHAPTER III

1. Luke 9:31
2. John 4:34
3. John 12:27
4. Paul Calvin Payne, "The Future Comes Creeping In," *Presbyterian Life*, June 23, 1951, p. 17
5. John 1:39
6. John 8:32
7. Matthew 1:21
8. Matthew 3:17
9. Matthew 3:16
10. Isaiah 53:2
11. John 12:24
12. Matthew 4:1
13. Matthew 9:12–13
14. John 10:10
15. John 5:40
16. Luke 18:9
17. Archibald Rutledge, *Life's Extras* (New York: Fleming H. Revell Co., 1946), p. 23
18. John 4:29
19. Matthew 9:18–34
20. John 16:33
21. Stanley Brown-Serman and H. A. Prichard, *What Did Jesus Think?* (New York: The Macmillan Co., 1935), p. 86
22. Hebrews 12:2
23. Spoken by Dr. R. E. Gaines and written down at the request of a friend, Dr. Romeyn Rivenberg
24. Matthew 10:28
25. John 3:16
26. John 14:27; 15:11
27. James Sutherland Thomson, *The Hope of the Gospel* (Greenwich, Conn.: Seabury Press, 1954), p. 77
28. Luke 4:18–19
29. Luke 12:14
30. Luke 4:28–29
31. Luke 19:10
32. Luke 15:18
33. Matthew 20:28
34. Luke 15:20
35. James A. Pike, *Beyond Anxiety* (New York: Charles Scribner's Sons, 1953), p. 63
36. Romans 5:8
37. 1 Corinthians 15:58

CHAPTER III (Cont'd)

38. John 18:37
39. John 19:10
40. John 18:38
41. John 8:44
42. Leslie D. Weatherhead, *After Death* (New York: Abingdon-Cokesbury), pp. 21, 26–27
43. John 14:3

CHAPTER IV

1. W. A. Smart, *The Contemporary Christ* (New York: Abingdon-Cokesbury, 1942), p. 37
2. Quoted in *Rediscovering the Bible,* by Bernhard W. Anderson (New York: Association Press, 1951), p. 70
3. Smart, *ibid.,* p. 35
4. John 14:10
5. Stanley Brown-Serman and H. A. Prichard, *What Did Jesus Think?* (New York: The Macmillan Co., 1935), p. 214
6. Matthew 5:48
7. Matthew 18:21–33
8. Matthew 5:45
9. Matthew 5:45
10. Brown-Serman and Prichard, *op. cit.,* p. 216
11. Ernest Ligon, *The Psychology of Religious Personality* (New York: The Macmillan Co., 1941), p. 23
12. John 14:1
13. John 10:30
14. John 14:9
15. James Moffatt, *Love in the New Testament* (New York: Richard R. Smith, Inc., 1930), p. 71
16. Matthew 6:26
17. Matthew 16:2–3
18. Matthew 6:30
19. 2 Corinthians 10:10
20. Jack Finegan, *Youth Asks About Religion* (New York: Association Press, 1949), p. 51
21. William Adams Brown, *Beliefs That Matter* (New York: Charles Scribner's Sons, 1928), p. 152
22. Emil Bruner, *The Scandal of Christianity* (Philadelphia: The Westminster Press, 1951), p. 26
23. John 3:9

Chapter IV (Cont'd)

24. Matthew 13:38
25. John 3:16
26. Matthew 28:19
27. John 4:24
28. John 3:16
29. Richard Roberts, *The Ascending Life* (New York: The Woman's Press, 1924), p. 40
30. John 15:12
31. Matthew 16:23
32. Matthew 18:23 ff.
33. C. G. Montefiore, *Rabbinic Literature and Gospel Teachings*, p. 222
34. Matthew 6:12–14
35. Matthew 18:35
36. Matthew 25:31–46
37. Matthew 11:28
38. Matthew 28:19
39. John 5:17
40. John 9:4
41. Luke 10:2
42. H. P. Van Dusen, *The Plain Man Seeks for God* (New York: Charles Scribner's Sons, 1933), p. 141
43. John 15:15
44. Regina Wieman, *Does Your Child Obey?* (New York: Willett, Clark & Company, 1940), p. 20
45. Matthew 11:30
46. Matthew 28:20
47. 2 Corinthians 5:19
48. Matthew 28:19
49. Matthew 28:20

Chapter V

1. Joseph Belcher, *William Carey, a Biography* (American Baptist Publication Society, 1853), p. 136
2. Acts 10:34
3. Mark 8:24–25
4. Charles E. Jefferson, *The Character of Jesus* (New York: Grosset and Dunlap, Inc., 1908), p. 18
5. *Ibid.*, p. 19
6. William Addison, *The English Country Parson* (London: Aldine House, Bedford St.: J. M. Dent & Sons, Ltd., 1947), p. 239

Chapter V (Cont'd)

7. George S. Counts and Nucia Lodge, *The Country of the Blind* (New York: Houghton Mifflin Co., 1949), p. 18
8. *Ibid.*, p. 19
9. Fred Bond, *Making Better Color Slides* (San Francisco: Camera Craft Publishing Co., 1951), p. 45
10. Matthew 5:22
11. Matthew 10:30
12. Matthew 10:29, 31
13. Matthew 16:26
14. Luke 18:17
15. Mark 2:27
16. 2 Corinthians 3:6
17. Mark 12:29–31
18. Philippians 4:8
19. John 15:4–5
20. John 2:25
21. Matthew 7:11
22. Howard Thurman, *Jesus and the Disinherited* (New York: Abingdon-Cokesbury, 1949), p. 106
23. Larimore Foster, *Larry* (New York: The John Day Co., 1931), p. 68
24. Howard Thurman, *ibid.*, p. 68
25. Martin Buber, *I and Thou*, trans. Ronald Gregory Smith (Edinburgh: T. & T. Clark, 1937)
26. Thornton Wilder, *The Skin of Our Teeth* (New York: Harper & Brothers, 1942)

Chapter VI

1. Matthew 6:10
2. Margaret Slattery, *Thy Kingdom Come—But Not Now* (New York: Harper & Brothers, 1939)
3. Mark 1:14
4. Mark 1:15
5. Matthew 6:33
6. Acts 1:6
7. John 18:36
8. Luke 12:32
9. Exodus 14:15
10. Matthew 25:14–29
11. 1 Corinthians 1:22
12. Luke 19:11

CHAPTER VI (Cont'd)

13. Luke 17:20–21
14. 1 Corinthians 1:22
15. Mark 12:34
16. D. Elton Trueblood, *The Predicament of Modern Man* (New York: Harper & Brothers, 1944), p. 53
17. Hillyer Straton, *Thinking Where Jesus Thought* (St. Louis: Bethany Press, 1945), p. 32
18. 1 John 3:14
19. Donald M. Baillie, *God Was in Christ* (New York: Charles Scribner's Sons, 1948), p. 205
20. John 7:39
21. Matthew 18:20
22. Matthew 16:16
23. Luke 22:32
24. Galatians 2:11
25. Acts 10:9–34
26. John 17:20–21
27. Matthew 16:17
28. Charles A. Ellwood, *The World's Need of Christ* (New York: Abingdon-Cokesbury, 1940), p. 26
29. Luke 10:3
30. Kirby Page, *Living Creatively* (New York: Farrar and Rinehart, 1932), p. 63
31. Matthew 13:44
32. Matthew 13:46
33. Margaret Widdemer, "Barter," *Ballads and Lyrics* (New York: Harcourt, Brace and Company, 1925)
34. Mark 13:32
35. H. E. Dana, *A Life of Christ* (Philadelphia: Judson Press, 1945), p. 79

CHAPTER VII

1. Walter Rauschenbusch, *The Social Principles of Jesus* (New York: Association Press, 1921), p. 105
2. Mark 10:42–45
3. Mark 10:31
4. John 12:24–25
5. 2 Corinthians 8:9
6. John 12:24
7. Norman Goodall, *One Man's Testimony* (New York: Harper & Brothers, 1949), p. 75

CHAPTER VII (Cont'd)

8. Philippians 2:7
9. John 13:3–5
10. D. Elton Trueblood, *Alternative to Futility* (New York: Harper & Brothers), p. 58
11. Jeremiah 9:1
12. Joel 2:17
13. Matthew 23:4
14. Matthew 12:1–4
15. Mark 3:1–5
16. Matthew 9:36
17. Matthew 23:37
18. F. W. Boreham, *A Late Lark Singing* (London: Epworth Press, 1945), p. 66
19. Matthew 12:50
20. George Bernard Shaw, *Saint Joan.* From *The Theater Guild Anthology* (New York: Random House, 1936), p. 383. By permission of George Bernard Shaw and Dodd, Mead and Co.
21. Luke 22:32
22. Matthew 28:20
23. Matthew 4:19
24. John 1:12